THE RUSSIAN GOVERNMENT
AND THE MASSACRES

THE RUSSIAN GOVERNMENT AND THE MASSACRES

A PAGE OF THE RUSSIAN COUNTER - REVOLUTION

BY E. SÉMÉNOFF

AUTHORISED TRANSLATION FROM THE FRENCH

WITH AN INTRODUCTION BY LUCIEN WOLF

GREENWOOD PRESS, PUBLISHERS
WESTPORT, CONNECTICUT

Library of Congress Cataloging in Publication Data

Semenov, Evgeniĭ Petrovich, 1861–
   The Russian government and the massacres.

   Translation of Une page de la contre-révolution russe.
   Reprint of the 1907 ed.
   1.   Russia--Politics and government--1894-1917.
2.   Jews in Russia.   I.   Title.
DS135.R9S3813   1972   320.9'47'08   70-97304
ISBN 0-8371-2632-0

Originally published in 1907 by John Murray, London

Reprinted by Greenwood Press,
a division of Williamhouse-Regency Inc.

First Greenwood Reprinting 1972
Second Greenwood Reprinting 1974

Library of Congress Catalog Card Number 70-97304

ISBN 0-8371-2632-0

Printed in the United States of America

CONTENTS

INTRODUCTION

SHORTLY after Prince Urussoff delivered his famous speech in the Duma, accusing the Russian Government of complicity in the "pogroms," a newspaper interviewer called on the late General Trepoff, and asked him what he thought of the Prince's revelations. " Urussoff has lied ; that is all!" answered the General with contemptuous curtness. It was easily said. How far it was true may be judged from this book. Here the crushing evidence on which Prince Urussoff's terrible indictment was largely based, is set forth in documents of undisputed and in - disputable authenticity.

It is, however, not as a vindication of Prince Urussoff that M. Séménoff's book is chiefly welcome. It is more especially valuable as a gallant blow struck for justice and humanity, and for the solemn enlightenment of the nations whom a politico-financial conspiracy of silence is slowly involving in the guilt of the Russian Autocracy. Hitherto the full truth has not been understood, partly because the available evidence has been published in newspaper fragments each of which has been lost in the quicksands of the public memory before the next has seen the light, but chiefly, I imagine, because civilised men and women necessarily find it difficult to accommodate their sober perceptions to the anachronism of so ghastly a crime. The Russian Government is Christian, and claims to be civilised and essentially modern. The Tsar is a nephew of our own King; his statesmen are gentlemen of culture and refinement, sometimes even of piety; and the nation boasts a crusading record as a bulwark against the Barbarian and the Infidel. True, they have their *défaillances* like other nations — a little worse, perhaps — and from time to time exceptionally ugly impulses have shown themselves in the stress of their civil and foreign wars. Blagovestchensk was a deplorable example. But from this to the charge formulated by M. Séménoff is a long, an almost incredible stride. For it is nothing less than that the political advisers of the Tsar deliberately and systematically use massacre as an instrument of government, and this not in times of armed conflict with the people or a section of the people, but as a normal expedient for assuring the stability of the Autocratic system! The world may well be forgiven for thinking that here is only some melodramatic imagining of revolutionary frenzy.

And yet if we reflect for a moment, the horrible thing is not so incredible after all. Montesquieu says somewhere in his "Esprit des Lois" that fear is an essential characteristic of Despotism, and cruelty its necessary consequence. No mere polish of manners, no actual progress in the arts of civilisation can modify this psychological deduction. On the contrary, every step in the political consciousness of the nations must increase the fears of the lingering despotisms and render them more dependent on the methods of defence appropriate to the barbarous epochs they have outlived. How true this is of Russia is shown by the history of the "pogrom" in all its modern forms. Its barbarous development has kept pace with the national struggle for liberty, and the consequent growing insecurity of the Autocratic *régime*.

The *idée mère* of the "pogrom" is the old maxim of unstable despotisms of which Catherine de Medici supplied the classic application in her incitements of the Guises against the Huguenots. *Divide et impera* was a more or less bloodless instinct of the Russian administration in Poland long before it produced its officially engineered St Bartholomews outside that region in the early 'eighties. When the normal political discontent became intensified by the economic mischiefs of Russian administration, the alien bureaucrats found it convenient to throw the blame on the Jews, and thus got rid of their own embarrassments by absorbing the refractory masses in domestic strife. Moreover, by encouraging anti-Semitism they were enabled to pose as the protectors of the people against the so-called national "parasites." It was not, however, until 1882 that these tactics, more or less local and desultory, were adopted

by the Central Government as a fixed policy.
Theoretical Nihilism had been gradually passing into the stage of revolutionary propaganda.
Loris Melikoff had sought to avert a catastrophe by persuading Alexander II. to grant
a Liberal Constitution, and it was only the
luckless assassination of that monarch that
prevented this sagacious project from being put
into execution. Alarmed by the peril they had
so narrowly escaped, the Reactionaries, with
M. Pobiedonoszeff at their head, counselled
the new Emperor to adopt a policy of the
severest repression. The hopes of the nation
had, however, been strongly stirred, and the
new *régime* encountered formidable difficulties.
Then it was that the new Minister of the
Interior, General Ignatieff, imagined the
"pogrom." With the assistance of the police,
the hungry *Kramola* was gorged with Jewish
blood, and thus for a time the revolution was
stayed.

The second stage in the development of
the "pogrom" is marked by the atrocious
massacre at Kishineff, and the sputter of
minor outrages which followed in its wake.
General Ignatieff's policy, which had become

a tradition of the Ministry of the Interior administered with scrupulous fidelity by his successor, M. Durnovo, had ended by defeating itself. The bulk of the Jews who had previously taken no active part in politics, timidly recognising all parties as their natural enemies, had come to the conclusion that only by self-assertion could their salvation be effected. A new revolutionary movement had been rapidly growing under the pitiless reaction of Alexander III., and into this the Jewish students and workmen threw themselves with enthusiasm. Since the 'eighties a remarkable change had come over the Jewish communities. By the side of the necessarily not very powerful Jewish "intelligenzia," a Jewish urban proletariat, largely industrialised, had been created partly by the harsh May Laws which had crowded the Jews into the towns, and partly by the protective policy of Count Witte, which sought to foster native industries as a corrective to the ruinously adverse balance of trade. A bond of union with the similarly situated Christian masses was soon established. It was cemented by the labour organisations which both sectio⸱⸱

found themselves compelled to organise, and by a common adhesion to social democratic doctrines. The entrance of the Jewish "Arbeiter Bund," founded in 1897 with some 30,000 members, into the Russian Social Democratic Federation, was the first sinister warning to the Government that its old policy of *brouillerie* had failed. For a time efforts were made to meet the danger by the ordinary methods of ruthless repression, but this only had the effect of transforming the labour organisations, including the "Bund," into frankly revolutionary and terrorist bodies. Then the "pogrom" was once more resorted to. The old theory of Ignatieff that the Christians were being ruined by Jewish economic exploitation was no longer possible in face of the loyal combination of the two proletariats. Accordingly, M. Plehve, who was then in power, substituted for it the specious cry that the revolutionary movement was an exclusively Jewish creation, and that the Christian "intelligenzia" and workmen had been seduced from their allegiance by Jews whose ultimate aim was to destroy the orthodox religion and establish a Jewish yoke

over the Russian people. Through the local
authorities and the subsidised press, the
country was flooded with manifestoes in this
sense, but still the people were difficult
to move. The police were consequently
encouraged to organise the bands of ruffians
known as "Black Hundreds," and steps
were taken to assure the benevolent neutrality
of the military. The massacres at Kishineff
and Gomel were the hideous results.

The third stage is illustrated by Bielostok
and Siedlce. As an appeal to the Russian
masses and a deterrent to the Jews, Kishineff
had proved a failure. The "whispering
humbleness" of the 'eighties had altogether
disappeared from Jewry. To Plehve's "Black
Hundreds" the "Bund" and the students.
with thousands of Christian sympathisers, had
defiantly replied by organising armed committees of self-defence in all the threatened
centres. For a moment it seemed as if the
"pogrom" had run its course. The resources
of the Reactionaries were, however, not
exhausted. They astutely resolved to oppose
organisation by organisation, and accordingly,
under the direct inspiration of the Court

Camarilla, the League of True Russians was founded by General Bogdanovitch. The primary object of this body was to use the " pogrom " for the defeat of the then impending Constitutional reforms. Its quarries were no longer the Jews alone, although it maintained the incendiary theory that they were the mainsprings of the revolution, but the whole body of Russian Liberals, including even Count Witte and his following of shifty opportunists. The Odessa and Kieff massacres of last November and the " pogroms " at Minsk, Tver, Tomsk, Rostoff and Saratoff, of which the victims were largely Christian, were the first-fruits of this new campaign. They were, however, not entirely satisfactory. In most cases the " Black Hundreds " of the True Russians had required military support. Moreover, the nation was unmoved except to indignation against the " pogromists," and this was strikingly shown by the Duma elections, which returned an overwhelming Liberal majority, to which every constituency patronised by the League of True Russians contributed its quota of deputies. New tactics were obviously required. At all

hazards and at least the Jewish section of
the *Kramola* should be extirpated. Accordingly it was resolved to hold the Jewish
communities collectively responsible for their
disaffected elements, and to force them by
fresh "pogroms" to deliver up the culprits
to justice. But this time there was to be no
dependence on ineffective instruments. The
fiction of an uncontrollable popular indignation was bluntly abandoned, and no trouble
was wasted on the organisation of "Black
Hundreds," although their aid was not refused.
The soldiers of the Tsar themselves, horse,
foot and artillery, were openly and shamelessly
employed in the butcheries and other nameless
crimes. This was the history partially of the
Bielostok "pogrom," and entirely of that of
Siedlce. The latter, indeed, was a regular
military *razzia* on a peaceful population, as
ruthless and obscene as the methods of
Oriental conquest at their worst.

Such, in its broad outline, is the life-history
of the Russian "pogrom" system. It shows,
as I have already said, that there is nothing
inherently improbable in M. Séménoff's con-
tention that massacres are a normal instrument

of government in Russia. They are, indeed, the natural impulse of such an anachronism fighting for its life. Once we recognise that there is a despotism in Russia which cannot accommodate itself to the modern spirit without becoming a negation of itself, all else follows. The Spinozists tell us that everything perseveres in its being, and that the effort by which it thus perseveres must be the actual essence of the thing itself. The essence of Despotism is arrogant greed, and its methods must consequently be barbarous. There is no common ground for reasoning between it and the Liberal forces by which it is assailed, and hence war is inevitable. In such a war the conditions must be dictated by the mediæval ferocity of the endangered Despotism. The natural result is " pogroms."

M. Séménoff, however, does not rely on any *à priori* arguments to establish his case. He gives us the documentary history of the "pogroms," and in many cases proves conclusively the causal connection between the central authorities in St Petersburg and the massacres. The evidence, of course, varies in value. For the periods of the elder

Durnovo and Plehve it is scanty, and in
the case of Ignatieff it is almost entirely
circumstantial. On the other hand, from
the time of General Trepoff's activity in
Moscow, and the foundation of the League
of True Russians, it is clear and irrefutable.
The connecting links between the Central
Government and the local authorities, and
the alliance between the local authorities
and the "pogromists" are convincingly
demonstrated. The value of this evidence is
not confined to the period with which it
directly deals. It throws a searching and
instructive light on all the earlier "pogroms,"
and helps very materially to confirm the
hypotheses of Government initiative in regard
to them, which have always been current in
Russia. If we compare the circumstances of
the "pogroms" in the 'eighties and nineties
with those of the last five years, we find they
all follow the same plan. In every case the
stimulus comes from without ; in every case the
local authorities are more or less active on the
side of the rioters; no redress is obtained by
the victims, and the identified leaders and
instigators of the massacres invariably go

unpunished, and in the most notorious cases are actually rewarded. The logical inference has always been that the strings were pulled by the Government for its own defensive purposes, but absolute proof was difficult to obtain. If now the hand of the Government has been flagrantly detected in all the later "pogroms," the hypothesis of its direct responsibility for the earlier outbreaks becomes a moral certainty.

One question in this connection remains to be considered. I have said that M. Séménoff has proved the direct complicity and responsibility of the Government. But who is the Government? On this question singularly disingenuous attempts have been made to throw dust in the eyes of the public. Count Witte and M. Stolypin have solemnly averred their ignorance and innocence of the "pogroms," and their assurances have been widely accepted. Sir Edward Grey even communicated them to the House of Commons as an excuse for carrying on friendly negotiations with the Tsar's Government. But who has ever said that either Count Witte's Cabinet or that of M. Stolypin con-

stituted the real and effective Government
in Russia? That they have been in a measure
aware of what has been going on is proved by
the revelations of M. Lopukhine published the
other day, and by the report of M. Makaroff
printed in this volume; but, responsible or
not, the chief blame is not attributed to them.
The reason for this is that they are, and
have always been, only the subordinates of
another combination, the instruments of an
"occult power" standing between them and
the throne, which is the real Government in
Russia, and on whose advice the Tsar chiefly
relies in all affairs of State. This was made
perfectly clear by Prince Urussoff in his
famous speech in the Duma. The existence
of this mysterious body is one more striking
illustration of the abnormally tortuous and
treacherous conditions of Russian official life,
which have to be taken into account when
we are challenged by the incredibility of
the "pogrom" system. Up to the time
of his death, General Trepoff, the confidant
and custodian of the Emperor, independent
of the ostensible Cabinet, supreme chief
of the police throughout the Empire, and

disposing of a budget of his own, was unquestionably the real Premier, and with him were associated General Bogdanovitch and all the most notorious pogrom-mongers in the country. They were the bulwarks as well as the Executive of the Autocratic principle, which in spite of the decorative acts of the spurious Government has no intention of capitulating to the national will. They were the champions of the corrupt and discredited bureaucracy, and it was they who organised and subventioned the massacres in the interests of Autocracy and Bureaucracy, and protected and rewarded the chief actors in them.

I must not, however, be understood as absolving the actual Ministers of all blame. That they can connive at, and even set in motion or prevent "pogroms" when it suits them is a proposition not difficult to establish. Instances have occurred within my own experience. When nine months ago preparations were being made to launch the great five per cent. loan in Western Europe, I was only prevented from repeating in print the criticisms of Russian finance I had contributed

to the *Times* in the previous year by undisguised threats of reprisals, in the shape of
"pogroms," communicated to certain influential friends of mine by authorised agents of
the St Petersburg Cabinet. Again, some
months ago, when a "pogrom" was openly
preparing in Odessa, and scores of appeals
for protection had been addressed in vain by
the Jews to the Ministry of the Interior, the
outbreak was stopped at the last moment by
M. Stolypin, on an intimation from one of
the Tsar's Ambassadors abroad that if it
happened, certain important diplomatic negotiations would be prejudiced. A singular
feature in this latter affair was that when
the Ambassador in question was first approached by the leading Jews of the country
to which he was accredited, he declared that
nothing could be done to stop the "pogrom"
unless the local Jewish communities took
measures to deliver up to the police the
revolutionists and terrorists of their race and
faith, and he advised his interviewers to
telegraph to them in this sense. This shows
conclusively that the type of "pogrom," afterwards so brutally exploited by the military

and police authorities of Siedlce, was actually known, approved, and made use of by way of threat by the Government and its agents before it was put into operation. After this, M. Stolypin's repudiation of responsibility for the massacre at Siedlce and his protest that it was an exclusively local outburst in which the authorities acted on their own misguided initiative, must be looked at a little askance; especially when we remember that so far nobody had been even reprimanded in connection with it.

Abominable as has been the conduct of the Russian Government, I cannot help thinking that the saddest feature in this tragic story is, after all, the attitude of the Governments of Western Europe. They are to a great extent participants in the terrible responsibility which has been traced so convincingly to the unscrupulous advisers of the Tsar. But for their complaisance the "pogroms" never could have continued so persistently, and certainly never could have developed into the infamous form they have most recently assumed—openly managed and prosecuted by the uniformed servants of the

State. The blunted moral sense of official
Europe has been a substantial encouragement
and help to these high - placed massacre-
mongers. Of this there can be no question.
Years ago, when every "pogrom" was swiftly
followed by a blaze of indignation throughout the civilised world, the Russian Government was always for a time shamed and
intimidated, and the intervals between the
massacres were long, while their subter-
ranean organisation was rendered increas-
ingly difficult. To-day this deterrent has
almost ceased to exist. Many of the generous
leaders of public opinion are dumb because
of officially inspired whispers that political or
financial interests may be endangered if they
speak out. And this dumbness inevitably
begets popular callousness, and then im-
perceptibly passes into actual complicity,
in the form of patronage of high-premiumed
loans which are used to finance the massacres,
or of connivance at political agreements which
have the effect of enhancing the prestige
of the Tsar's Government, and hence of
strengthening it in its murderous conflict
with the nation—a nation "struggling to be

free." Small wonder that the "pogromists"
laugh at Europe, and now pursue their work
without intermission or disguise! But here
the victims are not only Russian Jews,
or even Russian Liberals and Revolutionists. The whole moral consciousness of
the free nations of the West—and not least
of England herself — is being degraded by
this officially nurtured apathy. We may
note evidence of it on all sides, especially in
the most widely circulated of the halfpenny
newspapers. A sort of Cossack cynicism is
gradually substituting itself for the great-
hearted impulses of the older generations,
and every tyro of political journalism now
lisps glibly of the infamous *raison d'état*, or
expounds it, like M. Jourdain's prose, without
ever having heard of it.

To me as an old Liberal, born with the
echoes of 'forty-eight ringing in his ears, and
piously reared on the traditions of England's
unswerving and unfaltering championship of
oppressed peoples, the policy pursued by Sir
Edward Grey in this respect has been pro-
foundly disheartening. I say this without
any consciousness, and I believe without any

trace, of specifically Jewish feeling, for it is not my co - religionists alone who are being outraged and massacred by the " Black Hundreds " and the Tsar's suborned soldiery, but very many Christian men and women as well. Moreover, the Russian Jews who have taken part in the revolutionary movement are asking nothing for themselves, but are fighting solely for the liberation of the whole Russian people, and in harmonious and zealous concert with them. Properly speaking, there are no Jews in this great struggle. Hence my feeling on this subject is exclusively that of an Englishman and a Liberal. It is because I think Sir Edward Grey has weakly eluded a great Liberal tradition that I find his diplomacy so disappointing. I render every homage to him for the skill with which he disentangled himself from the detestable plan of sending a congratulatory naval mission to Cronstadt on the morrow of Bielostok, but unfortunately this has not affected his larger policy of an *entente cordiale* with a Reactionary Government publicly convicted of the systematic massacre of its own subjects. That he has privately and *officieusement* expostulated

with the Russian Government is also true, and
I am grateful to him for it; but this has been
of little real use, seeing that it has had no
practical effect either in stopping " pogroms "
for good or in giving a healthy lead to
the mystified public opinion in this country,
which remains in ignorance of it. How this
state of things can be defended passes my
comprehension.

Excuses have certainly been suggested by
Sir Edward Grey himself, but they are of
the most transparent sophistry. Juggling
with the distinction between the ostensible
and the real Governments of Russia, he
assured the House of Commons last July
that "the Russian Government" was not
" responsible for the massacres," but, on the
contrary, " deplored them," and this, he im-
plied, justified Great Britain in cultivating
exceptionally friendly relations with the
Russian Empire. I will not dwell on the
disingenuousness of this plea, for the issues
it involves are too serious for personalities.
What I wish to establish is that it constitutes
a deplorable defection from the national
policy, and this may be best illustrated

by recalling the action of previous British Governments, both Liberal and Conservative, in precisely similar circumstances.

M. Séménoff in the following pages has called attention to the atrocities of King "Bomba" of Naples as a parallel to the "pogroms." What was the action of the British Liberal Government on that occasion? Like the Tsar, the King of Naples "deplored" the outrages, and disclaimed responsibility for them. He was defended by Nesselrode and Walewsky, and even Lord Malmesbury thought he was uncharitably judged. The British Government in alliance with France, however, refused to accept his excuses, and when amicable exhortation proved useless, the two Western Liberal Powers withdrew their Legations in order to mark their "disapproval of a system of Government with which it is impossible to maintain friendly relations." Generous-hearted men throughout the world applauded this action, although, curiously enough, the Russian Government officially protested against it. A still more striking illustration is afforded by our relations with Turkey, and it is especially noteworthy because it is nearer our own more practical times. In the early 'nineties there were massacres of Armenians organised very much in the same way as the Russian "pogroms." The Sultan "deplored" them, but this did not impose upon Lord Salisbury, who solemnly warned him that he held him responsible for them. Subsequently the Sultan, precisely in the same way as the Tsar to-day, decorated some of the most notorious authors of the massacres, whereupon Lord Kimberly, who had succeeded Lord Salisbury at the Foreign Office, organised a collective protest of the Powers, sweeping aside with disdain the plea of the Porte that the decorated officials were innocent. At that time Sir Edward Grey was Under-Secretary for Foreign Affairs, but I do not remember that he proposed to accept the Sultan's assurances or to conclude an *entente* with him, although the evidence against him was no stronger—indeed, not as strong—than that against the present Russian Government. If this procedure was right in 1892, why is it wrong now? The plea that in the case of Turkey we acted on treaty obligations

is an evasion of the issue. There were no
such obligations in the case of Naples in
1856, and even if there were, they would
not have affected the question of guilt or
responsibility, or of our moral duty.

The truth, of course, is that Sir Edward
Grey has found it convenient to ignore these
precedents and to close his eyes to palpably
hideous facts in the interests of an *entente*,
which to some extent he probably regards as
a Gladstonian legacy, but into which chiefly
he has been intimidated, like Lord Lans-
downe before him, by the stupid bogy
schemes of foreign policy now so popular
in this country. As a matter of fact,
a Russian *entente* was never an absolute
doctrine of Liberal foreign policy. If Mr
Gladstone was Russophil in 1876, it was
only because the Russian Autocracy was
less detestable to him than the bloodthirsty
Turkish tyranny of those days, precisely as in
1854, when Russia had succeeded in re-estab-
lishing absolutism in Hungary, and Turkey
had opened wide her frontiers to the Magyar
refugees, Mr Gladstone found the Sultan
more akin to him than the Tsar. As for

the bogy idea of forestalling Germany, it is as short-sighted as it is certainly pusillanimous. But even were Germany the danger she is represented it would surely be better to risk an intrigue on her part with Russia than to incur the ignominy of complicity in the blackest crime of modern times.

Never since the days of Castlereagh has a British Government ostentatiously culti-vated friendly relations with a despotic power engaged in crushing out the liberal aspirations of its subjects. And this tradition, be it noted by the cynics, has been justified by its practical wisdom as well as by its righteousness. Canning was no mere senti-mentalist when at Verona and Laibach he bravely set himself on the side of the struggling democracies of Europe, and dared the allied Autocracies to do their worst. In the same way we could well afford—indeed it would be good business even from the point of view of Mr Maxse—to make Germany a present of the alliance of the bankrupt and eternally discredited Government of the Tsar, so long as we secured the permanent affections of

the Russian people, whose eventual triumph is
as certain as that the day succeeds the night.
But English history affords us an even more
eloquent and impressive example than that
of Canning. I venture to commend to Sir
Edward Grey's Liberal and Imperialist medita-
tions the action of Cromwell in the case of
the "pogrom" of the Vaudois. England was
at that time busy negotiating an *entente* with
France, precisely as she is to-day negotiating
one with Russia. Nevertheless, she at once
flamed into righteous anger. Like the
Russian Government to - day, Mazarin "deplored" the massacres, and protested that
the Regent of Savoy was alone responsible,
although his subjection to France was as
notorious as the dependence of the Governors
of Bielostok and Siedlce on the Minister of the
Interior of St Petersburg. Cromwell promptly
rejected the French excuses, and refused to
sign the treaty of alliance until the wrongs
of the Vaudois were avenged. "To be
indifferent to such things," he said bravely,
"is a great sin, and a deeper sin still is it to
be blind to them from policy or ambition."
This was a finer, a more English utterance,

INTRODUCTION xxxv

than Sir Henry Campbell - Bannerman's
ambiguous "Vive la Duma!" especially as it
was not attenuated by any private explanations to the French Ambassador. England
had her way. The "pogroms" were stopped
and the Vaudois were reinstated, and Cromwell did not lose the alliance of France, nor
were the greatness and security of England
abated one jot.

I am sanguine and old-fashioned enough to
think that if something of the same spirit had
been shown during the last twelve months
by our modern Cromwellians, the cause of
humanity and freedom in Russia would have
been sensibly advanced, and the moral consciousness, as well as the Imperial prestige, of
the British people would have received a
wholesome and much-needed stimulus. I
am not so foolish as to suggest that we
should have modelled ourselves precisely, or
even approximately, on Lord Palmerston's
tempestuous interventions, but between them
and the unworthy course we have pursued,
there are many diplomatic means of dis-
engaging our moral responsibility of which
we should have availed ourselves. It is,

however, not too late to retrace our steps.
The constitutional struggle in Russia still
continues, and the free nations of Europe, now
happily allied, owe it to themselves that, with
due regard to the *convenances* of diplomatic
intercourse, the natural bias of their sym-
pathies shall not be obscured or misrepre-
sented. I trust that this book may help in
some small degree to awaken the emancipated
Liberalism of the West to a sense of the
sacred duty imposed upon it by its own
happy conquests and its past traditions.

LUCIEN WOLF.

THE POGROMS

CHAPTER I

THE ORIGIN OF POGROMS

I COMMEND these accusing pages to the attention of my contemporaries. They will find therein faint echoes of the lamentations, the weeping, and the death cries which during the last three years have filled a part —the greater part—of Europe. They will also find a summary, imperfect perhaps, but faithful and conscientious, of the bill of indictment which the independent journalists and writers of all civilised countries are drawing up against the Russian Autocracy for the use of the historian of our times, from the early days of Kishineff, ever memorable and yet thrown into the shade by the whole-sale massacres compassed by the Russian Counter-Revolution at St Petersburg on 22nd

1   A

January 1905 : by the outrages in the Caucasus and the Baltic Provinces; by the repressive expedition of the ill-omened General Rennen-kampf in Siberia, and in the very heart of Russia, in Moscow and the neighbourhood, by the bloody work of the Dubasoffs, the Mins, the Rimans and the other infamous officers and soldiers of the Semenoff regiment; by the pogroms, the conflagrations, the pillaging, the outrages, the bombardments, the devastations of Odessa, Cronstadt, Sevastopol, Vladivostok, Minsk, Tver, Tomsk, Rostoff, Saratoff, Kieff, Kursk, Vologda, etc., etc—in all, upwards of three hundred places, small and large, and finally — the other day — by Bielostok — Bielostok, where the blood still flows—at the moment of writing these lines — where the military, faithful to the Government and the orders of its leaders, aids and protects the " black bands," organised by the subordinates of Trepoff, by the heads of the local police, and by the agents of the Union of True Russians, directed by General Bogdanovitch; where the dead bodies of the Jews, on account of their number, remained long unburied, and where outraged young girls could be seen flitting about like unhappy phantoms, seeking their murdered or vanished parents. But what the reader will chiefly find in this little book are the official documents, the actual facts, taken from life in the streets, the public places, the barrack-room, and the court of justice. These documents and facts are more eloquent, more convincing than the most laboriously, most conscientiously composed dissertations.

The future historian will have the advantage of a better perspective, more leisure for reflection, above all, more *sangfroid* and calm serenity for pronouncing judgment upon the whole of the Russian Revolution and Counter-Revolution. He will be able to paint in the whole picture of the organisation of the Counter - Revolution by the Autocracy. He will discover and bring to light all the details of the plot. I shall be happy if the present collection of documents and facts may prove of service as a finger-post, if not as a guide.

In awaiting the judgment of history, however, I can affirm, without fear of being shown to be wrong by the revelations of the future, that the following pages give their author the right to state now and henceforth that the pogroms are the work of the organised Counter-Revolution, the work of the representatives and agents of the dying Autocracy.

In its death throes this abject *régime*, which dates from the time of Peter the Great's successors, is committing crimes and horrors which exceed anything recorded of other absolute governments under similar conditions.

Nowhere in effect, neither in France in 1789 nor in Germany and Austria in 1848-49, have absolute monarchies had recourse to such methods as *pogroms*. History offers only one analogy.

We find, indeed, something approaching the *pogrom* organised by the Tsar's dying government in the kingdom of Naples in 1779, and during the first quarter of the nineteenth century, when the Ruffos[1] and the De Canosas[2] — due regard being had to the difference in time and extent — organised

---

[1] See "Histoire des Peuples et Révolutions," by Leynadier, vol. iv. chap. iii pp. 114 *et seq.*

[2] *Ibid.* vol. iv. pp. 150 *et seq.*

massacres, not of Jews, but of Radicals,
Liberals, Carbonari and Francophiles, with
an object and in a spirit similar to those
animating Ignatieff, Plehve, Trepoff, and
Bogdanovitch.

Professor Tarlé—himself one of the victims
of the Counter-Revolutionists, who seriously
wounded him at a manifestation in St Petersburg last year — explained this analogy (in
a lecture delivered in Russian on 17th June
last in the hall of the Geographical Society
of Paris) by the fact that the absolutism of the
Bourbons of Naples, like that of the Romanoffs,
had a long and gradual dissolution. The
duration of this decomposition, of this slow
decay, so contrary to what has happened in
other countries, thus afforded the two absolute governments the time and opportunity for
preparing these savage means of resistance.
Professor Tarlé was right in drawing this
comparison, but there are other more
immediate causes, political and social, which,
moreover, he does not ignore; and these are
the chief factors in the organisation of Russian
pogroms, which explain their periodical re-
currence during the past twenty-five years

and their intensity during the last few months.

The authorities have many reasons for perpetrating the Jewish pogroms, said the heroic *Nasha Jizn* (No. 465). Besides the immediate delight in sheer cruelty, besides the primitive incentive of cupidity, there is also the sentiment of vengeance against the Jews for the revolutionary work done by their more advanced members, as well as the desire to terrorise them by the horror of physical and moral destruction, to humiliate them by the desperate necessity of appealing to the oppressor for protection. The infernal design of poisoning the masses incited by the venom of violence, depravity, and authorised crime counts also for a great deal, as does likewise the plan of suppressing whatever civilisation they have so painfully acquired. Being transformed into wild beasts, they are rendered innocuous to the existing *régime* in proportion as they become a menace to social life.

There is also, at the same time, the hope of turning one people against another, one nationality against another, one class of the

population against another — and of thus
obscuring political and social discontent by
substituting for it national hatred.

Yet other ideas presided over the organisation of pogroms. It was very much to the
interest of the Government to cite to Russia
and to Europe the savagery of its bands of
hooligans as a proof of the patriarchal
barbarism of the masses of the Russian
people.[1] "How can you give rights or
liberty to such people?" they said to Europe,
and at the same time they declared to Russia,
by means of pogroms: "The Counter-Revolution is at work—the nation will exterminate
you Jews and Intellectuals — all you *Kra-
molniks* (revolutionaries)." And this spectre
of the Counter-Revolution, looming through
the conflagrations and devastation of the
pogroms since those terrible October days,
sends a thrill of terror through the stoutest
heart.

But the hooligans, the "black bands," all
the obscure forces of oppression, vanish little

---

[1] "Give a constitution to the rabble of Kishineff!" exclaimed
Plehve to the editor of the *Neues Wiener Tageblatt* (26th July
1903).

by little before the enlightened, revolutionised masses, responding to the appeals of liberty and justice, to the warming rays of the rising sun of a new life. The people itself entered at last upon an open struggle with Autocracy, and then the authorities gradually evolved new methods of defence, more and more terrible, more and more menacing.

The "populace," the "black bands," no longer suffice for attacking the "dangerous populations," and especially the most dangerous of all, the unhappiest, the most oppressed, the most humiliated, the most persecuted — the Jewish population. Since Odessa, in October and November 1905, it is not only the hooligans, the black bands, who perpetrate pogroms, it is the public force itself, it is the military and the police who accomplish this work. What a distance we have travelled since Kishineff!

"The pogrom of Bielostok is hardly a pogrom, it is a military expedition," said the *Nasha Jizn*, and it was right. Yes! the pogroms assume more and more the form of punitive expeditions, such as those which devastate the Baltic Provinces, or the

Caucasus. And here we touch upon a new aspect of the Counter-Revolution—its international side.

We cannot indeed forget the solidarity existing between European financiers and the Tsar's *régime*, to which they have advanced so much money, the money of others; or the solidarity of capitalists who have great investments (industrial, commercial, and financial) in Russia. We cannot forget, either, the political and diplomatic combinations, thanks to which the massacres could be carried on in broad daylight, without the governments of the "civilised countries" raising their voice, as they did not only against the massacres in Turkey, but even against the excesses of the Bourbons of Naples more than three-quarters of a century ago.

On the contrary, the German Government and the Government of Republican France, to mention no others, supported and continue to support the Russian governing class morally and by other methods. And the personal relations of a Minister of Foreign Affairs of the great Republic, *amie et alliée*, with one of the principal organisers of pogroms, then

B

chief of the Russian Secret Police in Paris, was one of the minor scandals of this alliance, a scandal which will never be effaced from the reputation of this new-fashioned minister of a great democratic state.

I will not, however, dwell further on the responsibility which the "civilised" world assumed, and still assumes every day, in not taking sides with a nation struggling *for civilisation* against a *régime* which only subsists upon massacres. I will revert later on to the mistaken calculation which the civilised world makes in persevering in this immoral and infamous attitude. I am now in a hurry to start on the history—as succinct as I can possibly make it — of the Jewish pogroms in Russia for the past quarter of a century.

It will be seen from the facts and documents I shall quote that the origin of Jewish pogroms (and non - Jewish also) is clearly traceable to the Russian Government, who used them as a means of combatting the Revolution. To those of my readers who are interested in the Jewish Question in Russia, I would recommend the pamphlet of

M. André Mater, "Le Juif Russe," and the
thesis of M. Allemand,[1] declined at first and
afterwards accepted by the Faculty of Law
in Paris, the best work of the kind I know
of in French, which, by the conciseness and
trustworthiness of its information, will long
remain the best exposition of the problem.
As regards myself, in order not to exceed
the limits of the task I have set myself, I
will only touch upon this portion to the
extent that may be necessary for the elucida-
tion of the subject of my work.

[1] See Appendix.

CHAPTER II

THE policy of the Russian Government towards the Russian Jews has assumed, during the last twenty - five years, such a character of oppression and barbarity that we may well say it has no parallel among the wrongs that afflict humanity.

This is the reason why, some ten years ago, the best-known Russian journalists and writers presented a petition to the proper authorities requesting the Government to repeal the laws and administrative measures, restrictive and irritating, often cruel and inhuman, which the Autocracy has inflicted upon a population of five to seven million souls, particularly since the accession of Alexander III. Likewise, during the university disturbances of recent years, the students have always placed in the first rank of their demands the admission of Jews to the universities, and the abolition of the barbarous and stupid limitation of the "percentages."

Since the reign of Alexander III. the number of Jews admitted to the universities in the course of a year has been restricted to from three to ten per cent. of the total number of students. This is the case even in the towns and districts where the Jews form a notable proportion of the urban population, if not the actual majority. The same percentage limits their admission to the high schools—truly a monstrous state of affairs. I beg my readers to imagine for themselves the position of families whose children have reached the scholastic age—middle-class families, or those in which the father follows a liberal profession, and who see suspended over their heads the Damocles sword of the percentage. How the innocent little children are overworked in order to reach the coveted standard, for out of ten or even one hundred only three or four are allowed to pass! The others are rejected without pity. What misery, what struggles, what intrigues, and—

to be frank—what bribes in order to obtain the favour of being among the successful few! And what tears, what unhappiness, what tender lives ruined, poisoned for ever!

Then again, once through the high school, what efforts to obtain the *excellence*, the gold medal which procures an additional chance in the *percentage* for the university! Here, too, what lives are broken, what tears are shed! And how many young persons of both sexes are obliged to exile themselves and go to foreign universities! Some are able to go, but what of those who cannot?

Until the accession of Alexander III. the Jews, though deprived of the few rights possessed by other "subjects," still enjoyed certain "privileges," which rendered their existence relatively bearable, and justified them in hoping for a happier future, which would permit them, by dint of work and education, to assimilate themselves more or less with the other "faithful subjects" of the Empire. As Jews they had no "right of domicile" except in the governments of the west and south - west of European Russia; but the possession of university diplomas, the completion of military service, and the payment of the dues of the "First Guild," conferred upon them the right of living everywhere. While fulfilling all their duties to the State, they could not, it is true, obtain promotion in the army or in Government service; yet under Alexander II. there were two or three cases of Jews being promoted to the rank of officer. There were even army doctors who were promoted to Acting Councillors of State, corresponding with the rank of general. There were Jewish artisans, and even some employés in the municipal services of the towns outside the Pale of Settlement— this modern ghetto, *sui generis.*

The Jewish intellectuals assimilated themselves more and more with those of Russia in general, and in the 'seventies, especially in the great university towns and among the most educated classes, this assimilation was well-nigh complete. The movement of ideas, art, science, and literature included some remarkable names amongst the Jews. I do not speak merely of those who, like A. Rubenstein or the learned Orientalist Chvolson, were for one reason or other counted among the

converts, but of such names as Orchansky
(civil law), Antokolsky (sculptor), Levitan,
(painter), Minsky (poet, who tends, unfortunately to mysticism), Mme. Hinn (prose
writer), Morgouliss (journalist), etc. As for
the revolutionary movement before the war,
the Jews had thrown themselves into it with
enthusiasm, contributing even their blood to
the outburst of liberty during the last thirty
years, and the names of Zoundelevitch, Hessia
Helfmann, Betia Kaminsky, Mlodetsky,
Vittemberg, Kogan-Bernstein, Leckert, and
others, are venerated as martyrs by all who
struggle for liberty in Russia.

The accession of Alexander III. was marked
by a reversion to the reactionary policy of
Nicholas I. in home politics, and the change
particularly affected the condition of the
Jews.

When, after the first hesitation, Alexander
III., under the influence of Pobedonostseff
and Katkoff, turned definitely to reaction, he
recalled Dmitry Tolstoy, soon to be replaced
by Count Ignatieff at the Ministry of the
Interior. This was the period during which
all the preoccupations, all the acts, all the

measures of the Government were concerned with a single object—the strangling of the " Cramola " — that is, of the revolutionary movement. One of the methods devised by these eminent statesmen was Jew-baiting. The orthodoxy of Pobedonostseff and the obscurantism of others took firm root in the obtuse brain of Alexander III., and it was easy to prove to him that Judaism was a menace to orthodoxy, and that the Jews filled the ranks of the revolutionary party.

Then arose a Judeophobia, a savage, a ferocious anti-Semitism. As the Turks in Armenia set loose the Kurdish hordes upon the Christian population in order to reduce the number of Armenians, so the Ignatieffs devised the anti-Semitic riots of the 'eighties and 'nineties. It was necessary to divert the attention of the people from their discontent, and to canalise it against the Jews. Disturbances broke out. Many of my readers will assuredly remember the accounts which appeared in the papers of the time. Even in France the subject was discussed. Some, like M. Flourens, dishonoured themselves for all time by calling these atrocities simply

C

police precautions; others, however, narrated the story with a simplicity, with an eloquence which was truly heart-breaking. Read, for instance, the account of the troubles at Lodz (from the 2nd to the 10th of May 1892), given by Jules Huret in the *Figaro*, and you will have a slight idea of the events of which I speak.

I will take the liberty here of quoting the final passage in Jules Huret's article:

" 'You are interested, then, in these unfortunate people, Monsieur?' asked an old Jew to whom I was introduced by a mutual acquaintance at Lodz. 'You knew, doubtless, that many more Jews were killed on that and the following day and many others wounded. The exact number was never known, because they took care to conceal it, but I saw several, yes, several!'

" 'About how many?' I asked.

" 'About fifteen in my district. Neighbours said more, but there were still others in the town. A woman, a neighbour, was violated, and lay half dead between her two young children, who were crying. I was miserable enough myself (his only son had been slain), but I went to her to try and help her a little. It was horrible, Monsieur, horrible!'

" 'How do you account for it all?'

" He shook his head.

" 'We cannot account for it. *They are told* that it is the fault of the Jews that they are unhappy, and they believe it . . . *and then they feel themselves sustained, encouraged.* You understand? There are many manufacturers at Lodz—yes, certainly there are many—who exploit their workmen, but the people who exploit them are Christians as well as Jews. Anyway, why do they attack the poor Jews, like ourselves, who have such difficulty in gaining a livelihood—yes, every bit as much as they? For example, I myself worked to the very last day, as long as I could. Now I am too old. My son, who was in indifferent health, wished to qualify for a lawyer whilst giving lessons, but at the very moment he received his diplomas it was decreed that Jews could no longer practise law. Then, disconsolate at having wasted his time at useless work, my son gave up his studies and was apprenticed to a tinsmith. Yes, Monsieur, to help us to live something had to be done. But he was intelligent, he was soon an experienced workman; he was beginning to earn a living. . . . '

" 'Don't they say that there are too many Jews at Lodz?' I enquired, to distract his thoughts which were ever recurring to the memory of his son, murdered during the anti-Jewish troubles.

" 'Yes, there are a great many of them.

But where would you have them go? They have been driven away from every place. They are authorised to reside in Poland, in the western Governments, and they come here. They must live somewhere. When all the Jews were expelled from St Petersburg a Jew of my acquaintance went to Gresser, the Chief of Police, and said to him: "You leave the dogs in St Petersburg. Well, I have eight children to feed, I have great difficulty in making a living. Let me remain here, and I will go on all-fours like the dogs!" "No," replied Gresser, "you are a Jew, you are less than a dog. Turn Christian."'"

This is how Jules Huret related his impressions in the *Figaro*, and yet pains were taken to avoid anything that might give offence to the Russian Government. It was at the time of the inception of the Franco-Russian Alliance, the glamour of which made it possible for the Russian Government to conceal from public opinion in France the horrors of the wholesale expulsions from Moscow and other great towns, which provoked an indignant and general protest throughout the whole civilised world.

I will not dwell upon the atrocities of the Grand Duke Sergius and of his right-hand

man, Trepoff, at Moscow, where the expelled
Jews were penned up in sheds in the bitter
cold awaiting their turn to be embarked like
cattle in trains *ad hoc*, where young girls, in
order to remain in the town, had to provide
themselves with the yellow tickets of prosti-
tutes, where children were separated from their
parents, wives from their husbands, and all
for the greater glory of Alexander III., the
Just and Peace-loving.

If the Sergius, the Romanoffs, the Gressers,
the Trepoffs, etc., were coarse and violent,
Count Ignatieff, one of the promoters of the
movement, was jocose and easy-going. A
Jewess, who with her husband had the right
to remain at Kieff, came and asked him, as
Governor-General of Kieff, to allow her old
father to stay with her.

" But, as a Jew, he has no right to remain
here," exclaimed the ever-gallant Count, " and
he must leave the town within twenty-four
hours."

" Where, then, Your Excellence, do you
want my poor old father to go ? Besides,
the law obliges me ' to maintain and feed

my father.' In expelling him you deprive
me of the possibility of obeying the law."

"Not at all, not at all, my dear madam.
In expelling him I only compel you to send
him monthly remittances wherever he may
take up his abode, and to keep the law at
the same time," replied the Count with a
charming smile.

The poor woman, in despair at the certain
death of her old father if he were expelled,
telegraphed to a well-known barrister at St
Petersburg, one of her relations and legal
adviser to the famous Liberal General
Kossitch, Military Governor of Kieff. Informed by telegram of what had occurred,
the latter obtained permission for the old
Jew to stay with his daughter. This favour,
procured with such difficulty, is in itself a
testimony to the tragedies enacted when the
Jews were expelled from the large towns in
Russia.

The Tsar Ivan the Terrible, having taken
possession of the town of Polotzk, found a
Jewish population there. "What is to be
done with them?" he was asked. "Baptize
those who accept baptism, and drown those

who refuse," he ordered. The second
Romanoff, Alexis Mikailovitch, after the
conquest of Vilna, gave the following order,
extraordinary even for his time (1658):
" Expel the Jews from Vilna, so that they
may live outside the town." The daughter
of Peter the Great, the Empress Elizabeth,
replied thus to the proposal for increasing
the privileges of the Jews in order to
augment the State revenues: " I desire no
benefit from the enemies of Christ."
Alexander III., the offspring of a line of
tyrants, having always before him the bloody
vision of a mutilated Tsar, gathered up in
fragments from the roadway, in the midst
of *débris* of bombs, dead bodies, and terror-
stricken courtiers in the open streets of the
capital—was inspired by the spirit of his
distant predecessors in his policy towards
the Jews, as, in the rest of his internal policy,
he was inspired by the tyrannic spirit of the
days preceding the reforms of Alexander II.
It was, of course, impossible to drown whole
crowds of Jews any longer — manners and
customs had, after all, changed to some extent
—but to kill a few here and there, to expel,

to trap, to scourge (as at Vilna fourteen years ago), all that was permitted, and we have already seen what the Russian Government did at Lodz, Kieff, Moscow, etc.

At the time of the "anti-Semitic disturbance" in 1882, the Jewish youth of Odessa were divided into two groups. One party desired, with the Revolutionists, to transform the anti - Jewish troubles into a general revolt, the other organised itself to defend its co - religionists against the excesses and violence of the crowd, egged on, it is easy to guess by whom. The revolutionary scheme did not even make a start, such was its weakness in face of the popular movement. As for the Jewish students who attempted to defend their co - religionists, they were all seized and put on board a vessel lying in the roadstead "while waiting to be shot," as rumour ran, and the intervention of the notables of Odessa was required to obtain from the authorities the deliverance of these prisoners.

Those who have some acquaintance with history in general and that of the Jews in particular know that the hatred of the

Jews, the persecution of Jews, anti-Semitism in a word, in all its diverse manifestations, originates in high places either with the ecclesiastical authorities who fanaticise believers against the enemies of Christ or with the political powers who for political, financial, or religious reasons treat the Jews as outlaws. This has been the rule since the time of Constantine, Theodosius II., and especially Justinian and his iconoclastic successors, who were afraid of being considered judaizing heretics. In free and civilised contemporary communities those who have taken the place of the religious and political authorities of other days are irresponsible journalists and authors who stir up the masses with their incendiary writings. We know them and their mental condition, and we understand the regrets they cherish for the vanished Inquisition, with its *autos-da-fé*. Though happily not so powerful for actual harm, they are of the same mentality as the persecutors in less enlightened lands. M. Drumont once said to Jules Huret:[1] "Love the Tsar! of course

[1] "Enquête sur la question sociale," p. 214.

D

I do, seeing that he is an anti-Semite."[1]
The Tsar in question was Alexander III.

To drive out the Jew from all government
services, from all the towns except those of
the Pale of Settlement, from all the schools
if possible—that was Alexander III.'s dream.
And in this feeble and limited intelligence,
in this tenacious and rancorous mind one idea
took root—to reconstitute absolute power on
a basis of autocracy, orthodoxy, and populism,
to declare war without truce, without mercy,
against all that was outside this trinity. If
he had not come into contemporary society
at least two centuries too late even for Russia,
scaffolds and severed heads would have
covered all Russia, even before the actual
revolution.

In order to illustrate what we have just
been saying, the following story will suffice.
On one of the railway lines in the south of
Russia, the station - master was a Jew. It
happened to be an important station through
which all the Imperial trains passed on their
way to the Crimea. There had been several
changes of station-master, for the responsibility of this position was very great, especi-

ally in view of the fact that a journey of the
Tsar disorganises a railway just as much
as a railway accident would do, all the
trains being stopped and side-tracked, and
a whole army being posted along the route.
Our Jewish station-master was remarkably
efficient. He seemed neither to sleep nor
to eat, and kept unbroken order within his
radius, even during snowstorms. The whole
Court, all the Grand Dukes—to whom, moreover, he rendered personal services at times—
knew and appreciated him. Then came the
order of Alexander III. to expel the Jews
from all the public services. General Petroff,
unable to act contrary to His Majesty's
commands, found himself forced to discharge
the station-master in question, in spite of the
intercession of several ministers, Grand Dukes,
and other high-placed personages, who looked
upon his dismissal as a disaster for themselves
and for the railway. "The Emperor must
himself make an exception in favour of X——
since he will not become a convert," said
these great persons, and they arranged that
X—— should be presented to the Tsar on the
arrival platform, while travelling to Sevastopol.

Alexander III., who knew his "station-master" very well, was exceedingly amiable, and asked him several times if it was true that he was leaving Russia, etc. The other replied boldly that he was forced to take this step as, being a Jew, he found it impossible to earn a livelihood for himself and his family. There was a moment of general embarrassment, of painful constraint: the courtiers and the ministers hoped for a sign of humanity, of gratitude, of pity, or even of shame on the part of the Tsar. The latter hesitated indeed for some instants, but his fixed idea—the keynote of his reign—proved stronger in him than any other sentiment, and he ended by saying: "It is regrettable. A pleasant journey! We will write to our ambassador."

Twenty-five years of a more or less civilised life were thus erased from Russian history by this outrageous obscurantism. If this official anti-Semitism found an echo in the popular disturbances in the towns of south and south-west Russia, the example was also understood and acted upon by the middle classes, and even by enlightened circles in the pro-

vinces, where the division between Jews and
Christians became more and more accentu-
ated. How, indeed, could it be otherwise
when the governmental policy in this autocratic country of extreme centralisation
pointed out, as it were, a whole population
as fit subjects for the contempt, hatred, and
persecution of all who wished to indulge
their evil qualities? Thus, prevaricating
officials took advantage of it to coerce the
Jews and extract bribes from them on every
possible occasion; others showed their hatred
and their "loyalty to the throne" by all the
means that their position and natural brutality
placed at their disposal.

Listen to what the journal of Prince
Ukhtomsky, the *St Petersburgskya Vedomosti*,
said at that time, employing euphemisms in
order to conciliate the Censor:

" If the Government thinks it necessary to
limit the number of Jews in the schools, that
is its business. As far as you or I are concerned, this prohibition does not oblige us to
take any action against the Jews, nor does
it give us any fresh right, for the same
Government guarantees the personal safety
of the Jews, their protection from assault (?),

and many other things besides. In making these restrictions the Government has no intention of branding the Israelite as a pariah, a helot, or of forming the Jews into a class apart, to be abused and humiliated as much as possible. Nevertheless, in all grades of society there are persons who think differently, and this state of mind is nowhere so dangerous as in the schools. There, in the presence of forty or fifty children, the Judeophobes ought surely to keep their antipathies to themselves, but as a general rule they take the opposite course. I do not speak of the cases which are difficult to show up, as, for instance, where the master teases an Israelite more than a Christian, a Catholic Pole more than an Orthodox Russian, where antipathies manifest themselves quietly, in criticising the exercises or the answers given in lesson-time; but all sorts of practical jokes and coarse pleasantries are practised which arouse the deepest indignation. A professor of mathematics in a high school, who excited the enthusiasm of his listeners by his jests, always chose two or three particular boys as butts for his shafts. He never addressed those with a gift for repartee, but always fell upon the submissive lads, and woe to the Israelite who became his victim! If, for example, the pupil could not find the right solution of a problem, 'It is not algebra you ought to learn, but how to sell rotten plums,' the pedagogue would cry. 'Come home with me, and I will give you my old pair of trousers to sell.' Or else, 'Son of a dog, accursed Jew,' etc., or 'Soloveitchik Boris! Present, Onoufriy Nikitych. Your name? Boris— No. Boruch'—followed by general laughter from the scholars. These instances might be multiplied, but we would be ashamed to tell of the insults, the blows inflicted upon children whose hands and feet were tied (for at the least back answer on the part of the pupil, the same professor would report him to the scholastic authorities). One blushes with shame for these men, who have received a University education, and who formerly worked for human rights, for liberty of conscience and religion."

For a semi-official Russian journal to speak in this manner, the general situation must indeed have been disgraceful. Let my readers imagine to themselves what must have happened, not at St Petersburg, but in remote provinces, what no person could mention openly in Russia, and they will understand the cry of alarm given by the journal of Prince Ukhtomsky, at that time the friend of Nicholas II.

We have had since then bloody proofs of this propaganda, and of these legislative

and administrative methods of the political
police, propagated and inculcated by the
brute force of autocracy amongst the Russian
people.

It was in this political atmosphere that
in 1903 Plehve resumed, in face of the
revolutionary movement revived with greater
force than ever, the counter - revolutionary
method of pogroms, inaugurated, as I have
already said, at the beginning of Alexander
III.'s reign by Ignatieff,[1] who had himself
borrowed it as a means of government from
one of his predecessors.

As a matter of fact, the "anti-Semitic
disturbances" offer no new feature, having
always been a means of government for
Russian Tsarism.   Thus in 1871 the Governor
of Odessa, the German Kotzebue, furious
with the Jews for sympathising with France
during the *année terrible*, revenged himself
by starting the "disturbances" during the
first three days of Easter week in that year.

We have already spoken of the system of
Count Ignatieff at the beginning of Alexander
III.'s reign.   At the time of the "disturb-

[1] See Appendix.

ances" of 1881 and 1882, all the Jews at Odessa who had organised a defence committee were arrested. This was the first attempt at organising the " Self Defence." It was not until after the horrors of Kishineff that the Jews definitely adopted this form of the struggle for life against the savage hordes let loose upon the poor Israelite population, the houses of the rich Jews being then, though not now, guarded by soldiers.

At Balta, the " disturbances" in the 'eighties assumed a more violent character, thanks to the connivance of the administration and of the police. One of the prominent Jews of that town, M. Poznansky, then went to St Petersburg and bravely accused the agents of the Government. But he had to suffer for this imprudence. The Governor-General, the famous Drenteln, came to Balta, and, having called together the notables of the town, addressed them in this fashion : " Who among you went and complained to St Petersburg?" "I did," said the brave Poznansky. " Ah, so it is you, filthy Jew, calumniator, liar," etc. Abusing and threatening the assembled Israelites, this chief of

E

Bashi-Bazouks ordered his victims to keep quiet, to demand nothing, to accuse no one, not even to point out the houses of the pillagers which contained their stolen goods.

At Poltava, when the authors of the "disturbances" were being tried, the public prosecutor stood up and attacked the Jews.

The Governor of Tchernigoff was removed from office for having stopped the "disturbances" at the very beginning. And this was the moment chosen by Pobedonostseff, the Councillor of Alexander III., to assure foreign nations that religious tolerance reigned in Russia!

Several years later, the authorities of Niko-laïeff, having learnt that the Social Democrats of this Black Sea port were preparing to celebrate the 1st of May, organised an anti-Jewish "disturbance," but fortunately the workmen foiled this diabolical move.

In 1902 Count Shuvaloff, then Prefect of Odessa, actually told the Jewish working-men, "If the 1st of May is celebrated here, I will organise anti-Jewish disturbances."

In Paris itself, a few weeks before the massacres of Kishineff, one of Plehve's

agents called at the house of an Israelite
known to the Russian colony, and spoke
to him in this wise:—"You have some
influence with your co-religionists: prevail
upon them not to attack the policy of
Plehve. Otherwise your co-religionists in
Russia will pay dearly for these attacks.
M. Plehve will stick at nothing."

In this way did the hour strike for the
Israelites of Kishineff and Gomel.

CHAPTER III

I NEED not describe at length the horrors of the days of Kishineff, soon to be followed by those of Gomel. With Mr Michael Davitt of the *New York American* and the *Times* correspondent at St Petersburg, I was enabled at the time to establish in the *Européen* the full and entire responsibility of the government of the late M. Plehve for the planning of this first bloody proof of the organised Counter-Revolution.

Plehve himself showed that we had discovered the truth in our respective and independent campaigns. Not being able to reach the courageous American journalist, he expelled from St Petersburg the *Times* correspondent for the publication of the famous letter from the Minister of the Interior, encouraging the massacres of Jews, and he forbade, under a threat of suppression, the editor of the *Novosti*, whose Paris correspondent I had been for many years, to publish anything whatever from me, even under a pseudonym. Thus, I was unable to publish anything in Russia until the death of this extraordinary, grave-digging minister of the Autocracy.[1]

Whilst, however, I will not dwell upon the horrors of the outbreaks themselves, I am yet forced to recall the general plan, the established facts and the names of the principal organisers and workers on the spot, the whole proving the direct participation of the Government in the massacres of the spring of 1903.

After a campaign by Kruchevan and his collaborator Chtcherbane, in the journal *Bessarabetz* (subsidised even after the pogrom by the Government) proclamations were

---

[1] In this violence offered to the Russian press, he took advantage of a discussion which he had had with me in the *Figaro* (he signed his statements, or caused them to be signed, "A Russian," and I signed my replies "Nesvoy"), and of which he had no reason to be proud. Even in order to publish, during his lifetime, a reply to a purely literary discussion in the *Novosti* I had to have recourse to all kinds of subterfuges. — E. S.

issued of which the following is an example:

"FELLOW-CHRISTIANS,—Our great festival of the Resurrection of Christ draws near. It is many years since, put to death by the Jews, our Lord expiated by His blood our sins and those of all the world, pouring out in His mercy His holy blood for the salvation of all the nations of the earth, of us Christians as well as the adherents of other religions.

"But the vile Jews are not content with having shed the blood of our Saviour, whom they crucified and who suffered for them. Every year they shed the innocent blood of Christians. They shed it and use it in their religious rites.

"You have doubtless been told that at Dubossari they crucified a Christian youth whose blood they offered in sacrifice. Well, the story is quite correct. The authorities know it too, though they do not breathe a word in order not to excite our anger against these miserable, bloodthirsty men who should have been driven out of our country long ago. It is with reluctance that the authorities cause to be printed that there is no foundation for these stories.

"A similar case has just occurred at Kieff, where they bled to death an innocent child, and afterwards threw its body into the street.

"At the present moment, whilst we are pre-

paring to celebrate the Passion of our Lord,
they are drinking Christian blood among themselves. Brothers, we are overcome with horror
when we think of the number of innocent
Christian souls lost through them for many
years.

" This, then, is how this abject race befools
us Russians. And what harm they do to
our beloved Russia! They aspire to seize it.
They issue proclamations in order to incite
the people against the authorities, and even
against the Tsar-Batiuchka (Little Father),
who knows them for a cowardly, vile, and
rapacious people, and will not give them
liberty.

" They try, therefore, to provoke disturbances by which they hope to obtain more
liberties for themselves. Now, if liberty is
granted to the Jew, he will become master
of holy Russia, lay his greedy hands upon
everything, and there will no longer be a
Russia, but only a Jewry left.

" Brothers, in the name of our Saviour who
gave His blood for us, in the name of our
very pious Tsar-Batiuchka, who watches over
the wants of his people, and alleviates their
lot by generous manifesto, let us join on
Easter Day in the cry ' Down with the Jews!'
Let us massacre these sanguinary monsters
who slake their thirst with Russian blood!

" Act in such a manner that they will
remember the pogrom of Odessa, where the

troops themselves assisted the people. This
time, again, they will aid us, inspired as they
are, like ourselves, with the love of Christ.

"Brothers, lend us your aid. Let us
massacre these vile Jews. We are already
numerous.—THE PARTY OF WORKING MEN
WHO ARE TRUE CHRISTIANS."

"Make your visitors read this, or else your
establishment will be sacked. We shall be
kept informed of this by those of us who go
amongst you."

After having enlarged upon the famous
and false legend of the "Christian youth"
killed by Jews, arrangements were made by
the organisers of the pogrom to start it on
the Easter Sunday.

There were, however, isolated attacks upon
Jews as early as Good Friday.

On Good Friday two old men were beaten
to death, and on the Saturday, as the women
and children were returning from the syna-
gogue, they were attacked and the clothes
were torn off their backs. The police did
not interfere, and their agents laughed aloud
as they watched the rabble at work. When
the Israelites brought some of these black-

guards to the office of the 4th Commissioner of Police, the Deputy-Commissioner thus scolded the prisoners:

"Idiots! Why could you not have waited till the festival?"

What, however, operated upon the crowd in a terrible manner was the open instigation of the police. The commissioners and agents pointed out quite openly to the crowd the Jewish houses in their districts, and kept the murderers away from the houses which they had been paid to safeguard. Such protection could also be purchased from the leaders of the black bands. Thus the ever unctuous and obsequious head of police Osovsky, to whom an officer remarked: "I do not understand how the police can tolerate such iniquity," replied cynically: "If you do not understand, do not trouble yourself about what does not concern you."

The Commissioner Berezovsky, well known for his imbecility, on hearing an Israelite reproaching the police for looking on and doing nothing, shouted angrily: "Ah! wretch, you have the impertinence to criticise! Clear out whilst you are still alive!" And the

F

Commissioner Solovkine, always brutal and insolent, when a blood-stained Jew ran up to him shouting: "Help, they have killed my father and my brother!" apostrophised him savagely: "What are you howling for, Jew? They have been killed—well—what of that?"

Two commissioners were less brutalised. One of them was even indignant at the pillaging and murdering, but when he was asked why nothing was being done to prevent them, he replied: "I can do nothing."

Some tea-houses and pot-houses—*traktirs*— were lighted up all night, and the chiefs and leaders of the bands gathered there to arrange their movements on the morrow. The *traktir* of one Pantiuchka, in Gostinnaïa Street, served as their headquarters. It was from this street that they sent their scouts and agents in all directions. About one o'clock in the morning an officer who found himself with his patrol near this *traktir*, thought it his duty to inform the Prefect of Police that a suspicious meeting had been held there during the night. The Prefect of Police replied that he would take steps in the matter, and added that all being so quiet the officer might go back to barracks with his soldiers, and the police would remain alone at the place mentioned. On the morrow the man Pantiuchka was one of the most bloodthirsty leaders of the pogrom, and in one house alone his band killed five persons. His order, "Strike till you draw blood," resounded through the whole street. He was not even arrested.

At Kishineff no one doubted the culpability of the authorities. They knew the incapacity of the Governor Von Raaben, since dismissed from office, who was always led by his officials and his Deputy-Governor Ustrugoff, and never understood what was happening around him. The Deputy - Governor Ustrugoff, however, was a man of quite a different stamp. He was an old and active rogue who could deceive a dozen Von Raabens. An ex-clerk who had made his way in the world, an ardent anti-Semite and reactionary, he was at the same time a contributor to and censor of the *Bessarabetz*, and he played an important *rôle* in the preconcerted massacres of the Jews. A cunning old fox, he had no necessity for detailed explanations, and he knew exactly how the wind blew and what was being prepared in the background.

But the soul of the plot was the chief of the "General Safety Organisation" of Kishineff—the Colonel of Gendarmes, Baron Levendal. This sinister personage arrived at Kishineff two or three months before Easter. His mission was very mysterious. He was independent of the chief of the local Gendarmerie, as well as of the Governor; he occupied fine apartments, and had at his disposal a large contingent of secret agents. It was known, however, that the administration of the Gendarmerie attended to its business as usual, *i.e.*, traced political suspects, followed them and arrested them by means of its own agents and gendarmes, and without assistance from Levendal. Hence people were perplexed as to the meaning of the coming of Levendal. Why on earth have a "general safety organisation" at Kishineff, where there is neither a university nor factories, and where the population is always peaceable and quiet? Some explained the matter thus:—"A position had to be found for a penniless baron, and they gave him a sinecure." Others, more sceptically inclined, retorted : " Why, then, such a swarm of secret agents, amongst whom, it is said, there are even women ? " So the mission of Levendal remained a mystery up to Easter, and it was only during the massacres that many people recognised the agents of Levendal amongst the leaders of the pogrom.

One of the principal colleagues of Krucheven and of Levendal was the famous Chtcherbane, editor of the *Bessarabetz*, amateur police spy and rabid anti-Semite. He even donned for the festival of the massacre of Jews the uniform of the Institutions of the Empress Mary ! In spite of all declarations and attestations of witnesses against this monster he remained tranquilly at liberty.

Levendal was very dissatisfied with the manner in which the massacres were conducted. He considered it too clumsy. " With provincial agents, don't you see, one cannot obtain delicate diplomatic results, leaving no trace of the guiding hand. It is only with the trained and practised agents of the capital that one can work well." Levendal had counted on more successful results, on more highly-trained assistants.

The bands trained and let loose upon the Jews went further than the instigators had intended, and on the opening days Messrs Ustrugoff and Company lost their heads, especially when they learnt that, owing to the attention the massacres had attracted, Lopukhine, Plehve's deputy, was coming. Quickly they organised a committee of relief for the victims, under the auspices of Mme. Ustrugoff, and a shelter and eating-house for those who were without a roof and without food. Mme. Ustrugoff spent whole days in the shelter, and the Deputy-Governor himself came and caressed the Jewish children, whilst murderers like the notary Pissarjevsky tried to get into the good books of the Jews in order to avoid being denounced.

But the arrival of Lopukhine *restored peace for a very good reason.* The picture changed with his departure, for he left behind him the *mot d'ordre* : " Don't make any blunders by which you betray yourselves."

The committee of ladies under Mme. Ustrugoff, organised to relieve the Jews, as had been announced in its appeals, began to assist the murderers also. An agitation was speedily set on foot in favour of the *Christian victims of the pogrom*, and for the first time in the annals of Russian society, there sprang up a movement of sympathy for a colossal collective crime, and this manifestation was made with the authority of the Governor and the blessing of the Bishop of the district, who headed the subscription list with a sum of five hundred roubles.

The Jews, as well as the whole population, knowing that the massacres were organised by the Government, did not expect any justice, and, to begin with, even lodged no complaints, while the assassins and the pillagers sauntered quietly about the streets, and the above-mentioned Chtcherbane, while bringing in some wounded Christians, cried: "The Jews must be slaughtered." It was only upon the arrival of a *procureur* from Odessa, M. Pollan, that enquiries began to be made, but hardly had he gone than the old order of things returned. Arrested persons were set at liberty, and the assassins were allowed to leave Kishineff. The band of Albanians brought there for the work were sent back to their homes in Rumania with their stolen booty. The examining judge Freinat destroyed the lists of the killed and wounded which had been drawn up by Jewish surgeons. . . . The rest is known.

The sinister comedy of the trials at Kishineff and Gomel dishonoured for ever the autocratic "justice" which proved itself the accomplice and protector of the murderers.

As it was impossible to prevent the group of heroic barristers from St Petersburg and Moscow, as well as some of the best known in the provinces, from taking part in the legal proceedings, absolute liberty was granted to the Government agents and the counsel for the anti-Semitic prisoners to revile the victims of the pogroms, and to cast in the teeth of the Jews the usual Judeophobe insanities. Silence, however, was imposed upon the counsel for the miserable beings who had been pillaged, mutilated, and slaughtered. The result was that the light, which had been ready to burst forth, was securely hidden under a bushel.

The Government, which had already in its official *communiqués* made out the pogrom to be the result of a street brawl attributable to the Jews, and had before the trial disqualified the inconvenient witnesses, was delighted at the departure, by way of protest, of the counsel for the prosecution. Of sixteen barristers eleven withdrew after a moving and eloquent speech made by MM. Zarudny and O. Grusenberg, and five remained to collect evidence for future occasions.

There was no further need for the Government to restrain itself. At the Gomel trial its representatives took up an even more scandalous attitude. Indeed, as we shall see later on, they went so far as to publish in the *Government Messenger* the vehement and odious attack on the Jews, full of falsehoods, delivered by one of the counsel for the defence, with the object of justifying the anti-Semitic proclamations and appeals which were still being sown broadcast throughout the country.

It was no longer doubted by any one that the Autocracy was determined to drown the revolutionary movement in Jewish blood.

The tragic death of Plehve, who was to

G

" save the *régime*," compelled his " friends,"
his " inspirers " and his " inspired," such as
the Grand Dukes and General Bogdanovitch, to unite their efforts, and form a
special group. Energetic action by means of
this secret organisation commenced throughout the country from the moment Plehve
vanished from the scene.

CHAPTER IV

THE PROPAGANDA

THE propaganda was carried on everywhere, and nearly always in the same way. The tell-tale documents and facts vary only in a trifling degree, according to the circles in which the propaganda was conducted.

These documents, as well as the unanimous voice of the universal conscience, accused and still accuse the Russian Government of having been the author of the massacres which continue to soak with blood the Russian soil. The facts and documents which we publish further on show how the authorities organised the massacres.

Let me quote here what I wrote in the *Européen* for 10th June 1905:

"The enquiries into the recent massacres begin already to yield results which prove the culpability of the Government for the massacres of Baku, Kostroma, Rostoff, Odessa, Jitomir, Nakhitchevan, etc.

" The Government agents are organising terrorist leagues in favour of Monarchy at Moscow, Kishineff, etc., and proclamations bearing an official stamp are distributed broadcast among the population, calling upon them to massacre the enemies of the Tsar and of the country.

" The following appeal, signed ' Jarema,' was circulated for two or three weeks, and prepared the ground for the massacres of Jitomir, Simferopol, Melitopol, etc., just two years after Kishineff, with greater cynicism and audacity than ever. It was the military and the police who got the upper hand of the *samoborona* of Jitomir (free militia of self-defence), which, at this period, makes its first appearance in defence of the unhappy population against the black bands organised by the authorities.[1]

" ' Brother peasants ! During these two past years there have begun to appear proclamations in which the enemies of the Russian people attempt to sow in their midst the seeds of mistrust towards the Emperor and his government. Brothers ! observe that these proclamations are issued amongst the population by the Jews. You understand, therefore, which way the wind blows. The Jews by themselves would not dare to act

[1] See the *Européen,* Nos. 180 *et seq.*

thus if they were not encouraged by other
enemies of the Russian people. These
enemies are :—the Poles, who cannot resign
themselves to the fact that we are no longer
their serfs ; the Japanese and their allies the
English and the Americans, who began the
war ; and finally the Israelites. The foul
and hateful Jews wish now to dominate us.
There is a reason for this. The Japanese
have given the Jews money to annoy the
Russian people. The Poles have promised
them that serfdom will be re-established, and
that the Jews can farm out the churches,
public-houses, etc.'

" Then follow quotations from the Scriptures,
and reminders of the times when the Jews
were massacred.

" ' It is necessary that they should remember
those times. Jewry has eaten Russian bread
long enough. Now it is in the mood for kick-
ing. Down with such trash !'

" This appeal reached certain journals, and
the *Kieff Gazette* proposed to publish the
following statement :

" ' A certain person named Jarema sends
letters to the peasants. He tries to make
them believe that the Jews and the Poles are
the enemies of the Russian people. We trust
that the clergy and those who watch over the
moral welfare of the people will take some
action against this excitation of national
passions.'

" The censor, A. A. Sidoroff, 'withheld' this notice, promising a decisive reply in two days' time, after referring to the Governor-General. Two days later the notice was 'forbidden.' In this manner did Jarema find himself under the protection of M. Sidoroff and the Governor-General of Kieff.

" The censor, the Governor-General of Kieff, the local police in the person of its chief, Kuiaroff, and his assistant, Iarotzky (both of whom have since been executed by the Revolutionists), are the persons really responsible for the massacres of Jitomir, the chief town of Volhynia. The *Christian inhabitants* of the suburb of Malevanka addressed to the general government of Volhynia, of Podolia, and of Kieff, a protest against the 'authorities who have admitted these massacres.' The troops who *favoured* the massacres, and in the ranks of which the Christian student Blinoff was killed for requesting the commanding officer to stop the massacres — these very troops had been held in readiness there, as more or less everywhere, to second the efforts of the slaughterers.

" The *Poslednia Izvestia* of 31st May published a whole series of official secret documents emanating from the Governor-General, and addressed to the Governor, and from the Governor to the Director of the Chamber of Accounts, which contain perfidious insinuations against the Jews, and are all of a nature to show the necessity for an increase of the police force at Jitomir, at the expense of the Jews.

" In order to show my readers how the authorities themselves create an atmosphere of pogroms against the Jews in the western provinces, while the same thing is being done in the Caucasus and elsewhere against the intellectuals, I shall quote a document which emanates from the office of the Governor of Kovno, and is secretly addressed, under date 4th May 1905, to the Prefect of Police at Kovno, and to all the local chiefs of police. It begins by quoting the depositions of the Quarter - Master - General of the military district of Kieff relative to the appearance of Chinese ' who retail Chinese silk, a thing which never occurred before the present war with Japan.   Their appearance during the war, while not in itself furnishing sufficient reasons for affirming that they are carrying on a system of espionage in favour of Japan, provokes nevertheless suspicions in this direction, all the more as they were, *it appears*, in intimate relationship with a part of the Jewish population.'

" And the circular concludes by pointing out the necessity for being on the watch, for keeping the Government well informed, and for taking measures in case of necessity.   The document bears the signature of M. Verevkine, Acting Governor, and of his Chef de Cabinet, M. Briling.

" I cannot prolong indefinitely the quotations of official documents proving the guilt of the authorities who create this atmosphere of massacres which pervades all Russia at the present time.

" I will, however, quote extracts from two letters of a soldier, Ivan Iankofsky, to his people, relating to the massacres of Jitomir, in which he had participated on the 6th, 7th, and 8th of May 1905.

" In his first letter he says that it was the Jews and the Russians who, with revolvers and rifles, 'have made a great revolt, a veritable war,' and he puts the number of wounded amongst the soldiers at 200.

" ' We are not going to the Far East. We do not know what is going to happen. There is a telegram from the Tsar to say that we can shoot down the Jews.'

" Who spreads such rumours amongst the soldiers ?

" In another letter from the same person to his father, sending good wishes for the Easter Festival, he describes the disorders and destitution in the town. No bread, nothing to eat.

" ' And who began the revolt ? The Jews, and more than 150 of them have been killed. A whole regiment of soldiers is parading the town, and yet they cannot be subdued. It is the *Katzapes* (people from Moscow) who slaughter the Jews. But it is a command of the Emperor's given long ago. If you kill a Jew it does not matter, but if you strike one and do not kill him you are placed upon trial, for if he is killed he will not rebel any more, but if you have not killed him it is yourself who are the cause of the disorder. On the 5th May a telegram arrived ordering us to strike every Jew we seized as much as we liked, but not to let them go alive.   God! What scenes are happening in this town!   It is impossible to describe them.   Day and night they drag the killed to the cemetery, and the wounded to the hospital, and others are thrown over the cliffs, and one does not even find their bones in the water.   We only sack the shops of the Jews.   If we find a *livowir* (revolver) in a Jew's house, we cut off his head and hoist it on a pole, and say that we have taken a Jewish flag.   Do the same with yours.'"

In order to understand this state of mind in a soldier before the great pogroms of October and November 1905, we invite our readers to give their attention to the following excerpt from the official journal of the Constitutional Democratic party, the *Retch* of 2nd May 1906, which shows that the propaganda and the activity of the murderers still continue in the same spirit and the same direction.

H

This is the fragment :—

A Jewish soldier of the 38th Regiment of Tobolsk, in garrison at Warsaw, sends the following declaration :

" Our colonel made this speech to his soldiers the other day.

" ' Soldiers ! Russia, our Little Mother, is passing through sad times. Wicked people, disturbers of the peace and Socialists, wish to divide up our country, and have even already begun to excite our brave troops, spreading their doctrine amongst the faithful servants of our Little Father, the Tzar. Most of these agitators are Jews and Poles.

" ' Remember then, my brothers, who your enemies are, and exterminate them everywhere, whenever you have the opportunity. If in chasing a rioter (*kramolnik*) you kill, in firing at him, another by mistake, you have nothing to fear ; on the contrary, you will still be rewarded. Remember that we are living in a state of siege, and the more each of you exterminates his enemies, the greater will be his reward. Remember, too, that our internal enemies, the Jews, Poles, and Socialists, are far more dangerous than our external enemies.'

" After this speech, the adjutant of the regiment advanced and called out :

" ' Those who can read and write, advance two steps !'

" Fourteen Jews and four peasants left the ranks.

" ' Jews ? ' cried the adjutant.

" ' Israelites ! ' replied the soldiers.

" ' The same thing !   Clear out ! '

" The company commander arrived that evening at the barracks and read out an article from the *Moskovskya Vedomosti,* which he accompanied with these words :

" ' All the misfortunes which have befallen our country come exclusively from the Jews, who drink our blood, and yet pass for friends of the moujik and the Russian working man. But do not believe it !   Mochka (a diminutive form of Moses, used in contempt)—he pointed out one of the soldiers—' he is your enemy, and I, a Russian and Orthodox gentleman, I warn you.   Do not believe Mochka !   Spit in his face ! '

" The soldiers surrounded Mochka and carried out literally the order of their chief.

" His patience finally came to an end, and when his *diadka* (instructor) approached him and began to spit in his face, he could contain himself no longer and boxed his ears twice.

" He was arrested, and at the present time awaits, in the military prison, the sentence of the court-martial.   We have no need to multiply examples to make our readers understand the mental condition of the soldiers trained in this manner with a view to further pogroms."

CHAPTER V

THE *Revolutionnaïa Rossia*, the *Iskra*, the *Poslednia Izvestia*, and other papers have published from time to time confidential official documents by means of which the military authorities provoked reprisals principally against the Jews, who were accused of all manner of misdeeds, and amongst others of "removing the rails" on the lines over which military trains passed!

All these facts, however, shrink into insignificance before the latest acts of the Government!

It was for the most part the *Novoïe Vremya* and other anti-Semitic papers which, on the approach of Easter, recalled the crimes attributed to the Jews in the circles of "true patriots."

This time, however, as the *Novoïe Vremya* was engaged in scoffing at the scientific men, the lawyers and the Jews, who "only demand a constitution for themselves," it was the *Government Messenger* itself which, as Easter drew near, and in the midst of a general panic among the Jews of southern Russia, took upon itself to make these seasonable provocations. With this object the official journal of the Government exhumed the report of the Gomel trial, that monument of insolence, of falsification, and of Governmental pressure, and published in a prominent place the speech *in extenso* of the anti - Semitic lawyer Chmakoff, *printing in italics* the passages most offensive to the Jews, pronounced by that barrister, thanks to the connivance of the president of the tribunal.

In order that my readers may understand the whole scope of the publication in the *Government Messenger*, I will quote some passages from the anti-Semitic speech underlined by the representatives of the Government to attract the attention of future murderers:

"The Jews have become so insolent that

they push Christian men and women off the pavement into the mud, and they mock at officers, calling after them *Sons of Mars!*

" The working men of Gomel are said to have complained to the commander of the 160th Regiment that 'the Jews take us not for men but for dogs!' . . .

" The massacres of Christians by Jews (!) were carried out pitilessly and principally by *blows on the head*, or by *knife-thrusts in the throat*, as we explain below, with an accompaniment of Jewish cries, ' *You are no longer in Kishineff.*' On the following day the acts of the Jews were still more insolent than usual, and their cries could be heard : ' *We have bought Gomel, it belongs to us!*' and at the same time they sang : 'The hour has come, and we have cudgels ready for the Christian dogs.'"

The rest is in the same strain! We shall see the results of this propaganda.

Keeping step with the official organ of the Government, the *Grajdanine* and the *Moskovskya Vedomosti* [1] openly preached under the benevolent eyes of the authorities the assassination of the *intellectuals*, while waiting for the " coming of a new Plehve or a new Araktcheieff" (a sinister despot and a

[1] See chap. xiii.

favourite of Alexander I.). At the same time
the police everywhere organised themselves
hand in hand with the *Tchornya Sotni* (the
Black Hundreds) with a view to the promised
St Bartholomew.

In the provinces the authorities were even
more insolent and more frank. Here is one
example from among a thousand.

The official Government journal of Ufa,
the *Oufimskya Goubernyska Vedomosti*, took
upon itself to excite the people against the
intellectuals. Shocked by this scandalous
official propaganda, a society in Ufa decided
to send a petition to the Minister asking him
to put an end to this dangerous campaign.
The petition bore a number of signatures of
members of the "zemstvos," doctors and
others, when it was brought to a merchant
named Boussoff for his signature. He refused,
and reported the matter to the Governor.
His Excellency demanded the name of the
person who had presented the petition to the
informer. The latter gave Dr Cheftel's name,
and he was sent for at once, cross-examined,
deprived of the petition, and thrown into
prison! Dr Cheftel remained a long time

in prison in spite of the collective protesta-
tion of the medical society of Ufa against
his arbitrary arrest, and in spite of the protest
of the public prosecutor himself. The latter
even went to prison to visit Dr Cheftel, and
said to him: "You have both the law and
myself on your side." The Governor, who
had on his side the Minister and the police,
laughed at law and justice.

It was in this atmosphere of provocation,
of partial massacres and of panic, reflected in
the independent journals — alas! how few
they are throughout the world — that the
culminating act of the tragedy approached.

Our desperate appeals in the *Européen*,
those made by "The League of the Rights
of Man and of the Citizen," "The Society of
the Friends of the Russian People" (in public
meetings organised in Paris, Brussels, and
elsewhere), passed for exaggerations.

The *Aurore*, organ of the French Minister
of the Interior, M. Georges Clémenceau,
published as a leading article in its issue for
9th July 1905, the following:

"REVENGE!

" It appears that the Russian Government is about to revenge itself for the humiliation it suffered through the revolt of the Black Sea Fleet.

" A massacre of the Jews of Odessa is being arranged.

" The precursory signs are not wanting for those who know what the Russian bureaucracy is capable of when at bay. Already a significant telegram of the *Agence Havas* insists upon the part played by the Jewish students, male and female, at the time of the mutiny on board the *Kniaz-Potemkin.*

" The correspondent of the *Journal* reports the account of a wounded revolutionary, who is said to have revealed the plans for setting fire to the Peresype and Moldovanka suburbs. Now those acquainted with Odessa know that these two quarters are inhabited by the poorest class of the population, the most ignorant, and the most experienced in the business of 'pogroms.'

" The *Echo de Paris* prints a telegram from Odessa of 6th July, which states that the police are discovering numerous bombs, especially in apartments inhabited by Jews. *The rumour goes that the Jews are going to be attacked,*

I

adds the telegram, *for the Russians abhor them, and hold them responsible for the recent disturbances.*

"That is enough. To anybody not afflicted with mental blindness, it is evident that the local authorities are making preparations for a massacre of Jews. They are preparing it because, if official Russia can accept the disasters of Mukden and Tsushima, it cannot accept that of the Black Sea. To the revolutionary demonstrations of sailors and soldiers who have *taken the oath of fidelity to the Tsar*, a reply must be made by a *spontaneous* outburst of loyalty from *true Russians.* *True Russians* will have recognised that the miscreant Jew has wrought all the evil. When these true Russians have learnt, and they are now being taught this, that the Jews keep bombs, that the Jews wish to burn down their poor dwellings, they will arise as one man to avenge themselves, to avenge the Tsar and the country. They will rise all the more readily because Odessa, a town of 400,000 inhabitants, conceals a crowd of vagrants who, under the paternal eye of the police, are always ready to commit theft, outrage, or pillage, assured as they are of doing so with impunity. The trial of the assassins of Kishineff is sufficient security for this.

"And then, since it is averred that the Jews of Odessa are effectively armed in view

of 'pogroms,' and since the police are aware
that the most advanced elements, from the
political point of view, are disinclined to let
themselves be slaughtered, the military who
will be there to re-establish order will re-
establish it as they did at Gomel: they will
fire on the Jews who leave their houses to
defend themselves, and the trick will be
done.

"The hermit of Tsarskoe-Selo will not be
personally concerned in this, but the satellites
who surround him and who try by fire and
sword to prolong the hunt, will know how
to saddle him with the whole responsibility,
for, in his capacity of Autocrat, he alone is
responsible.

" It is to be hoped that the projected crime
will not be accomplished, as it has been revealed
in time.   General Count Ignatieff, despatched
to Odessa with exceptional powers, bears a
famous name.   It is as celebrated in the
history of the Russian Jews as that of
Mouravieff is amongst the Poles.   General
Count Ignatieff must surely know that his
acts and deeds are watched by the whole
civilised world."

And the terrible days of October and
November burst upon the civilised world,
stupefied and terror-stricken, which had not

believed our warnings. . . . We will not
return to these horrors, which are still fresh
in the memory of all. We now approach a
document of prime importance which throws
a flood of light on these events.[1]

[1] See the *Européen*, December to January 1905-6.

CHAPTER VI

ORGANISERS OF THE MASSACRES

M. DE WITTE, who in his capacity of Prime Minister shared with Nicholas II. the responsibility for the massacres of last October and November, received from the well-known mine-owner, M. F. A. Lvoff, a memorandum revealing the inner workings of the organisation of the fateful days at Odessa, Tomsk, Kieff, Rostoff, Nikolaïeff, Minsk, Kishineff, etc. Those who disbelieved were very numerous. Others repudiated it furiously; yet others asked indignantly: " Is it possible that the Government through its agents can have gone so far?" But authentic information, eye-witnesses, telegrams, letters, even official statements arrived. The proof of the horrible fact, the fact which makes the blood run cold, is here; the whole world has learnt the truth and shudders with horror.

The author of the memorandum recalls the actions of Plehve's band. He had written before the war, on the occasion of the famous concessions on the Yalu : " It is not possible to play the Russian national anthem with one hand and to try the effect of a skeleton key on the Tsar's treasure - chest with the other." He tells us how this band of Grand Dukes, of generals, of Plehve's underlings, of provincial governors, seeing the danger of liberty, organised, after the well - known attempts of Kishineff and Gomel, corps of cut-throats under the form of patriotic groups, leagues, and societies, of which the *Russkoïe Sobranje* (Russian League) was the chief, their pretended object being the safeguarding of the person of the Tsar. The reactionary papers, for instance the *Novoïe Vremya*, published accounts of the work of these societies, together with telephone messages from Moscow, announcing that these patriots were already a hundred thousand in number, and would guarantee the personal safety of the Tsar. Under this disguise of patriotism and regard for the Tsar's person, these cut-throats in high places prepared a counter-revolution.

" The shame and the horror of the whole of Russia," says M. Lvoff, "originated at No. 51 Bolchaïa Morskaïa, St Petersburg. Here, in agreement with the Grand Inquisitors (nickname given to Pobedonostseff and the prelates who publicly preached the massacres of the ' intellectuals ' in Moscow, Tomsk, etc.), the former head of St Isaac's Cathedral in St Petersburg, now at the head of the general staff of the Black Hundreds, Lieutenant - General Eugène Vassilievitch Bogdanovitch, with the help of the patrons of the police and the Gendarmerie and the members of the *Russkoïe Sobranje*, elaborated the devilish plan of establishing Autocracy for ever in Russia through fire and sword. The heads of the army—their names are hated throughout the whole of Russia—took part in the plan, and all our governments behind the scenes (it is well known that there are several of them—the Grand Dukes, Ignatieff and Co., the underlings of Plehve-Stichinsky, Sturmer and Co., etc., also the volunteers of Autocracy, and Plehve's ' mongrels ') all gave their help."

The author goes on to enumerate the measures taken by these secret governments for a new massacre :—the proclamation of martial law in Poland, the rumoured meddling of William II., and the presence of his warships before Cronstadt, arbitrary arrests, distinctions awarded to officers and other leaders of the massacres, etc., etc. He recapitulates his charges in the following terms:

" I assert—and I am ready to stake my life on it—that under the auspices of the Gendarmerie a fighting militia (*Boïevaïa Droujina*) has been organised under the General of the Black Hundreds, Eugène Vassilievitch Bogdanovitch, and many of his colleagues of Moscow, Kursk, Tamboff, Tver, Odessa, Rostoff, Kharkoff, Ekaterinoslav, Tomsk, etc., with the benediction of Bishop Vladimir and others, and with the assistance of Plehve's followers and of the members of the Society of Banner-Bearers. For this purpose General Bogdanovitch has made frequent journeys to numerous Russian towns. In the month of September, in memory of Zoubatoff[1] and Co., the *Boïevaïa Droujina* was definitely constituted with branches under various 'platonic' names, but all retaining their sanguinary object. The success of the movement enabled General Bogdanovitch to

[1] The famous agent who, protected by Trepoff and the Grand Duke Sergius, founded the organisation of police spies amongst workmen, first in Moscow and then in St Petersburg, which resulted in the work of Gapon.

boast to the Tsar, that his militia (*Droujina*)
numbered 100,000 men, all ready to shed
their blood to serve His Majesty and their
country. Quite recently, in a report to the
Emperor, Count Witte declared that General
Bogdanovitch had lied, but if so he lied
in good faith, for although the nucleus of
the militia was only 6,000 men, many other
black bands were to have been provided
by the provincial 'centres,' for which the
leaders of this 'decorative' patriotism, such
as Kleigels, Neidhardt (and his brother,
the prefect of police), Moedem, Deduline,
Bogdanovitch junior, Sleptzoff, Stolypin,
Azantchefsky, Piler-Pilchou, Kurloff, Lopukhine, Rogovitch, Chirinkine, etc.,[1] had made
themselves responsible. There were 103 of
these upholders of arbitrary bureaucracy. Their
objects were:—to restore the prestige of the
Autocracy shaken by the scandals of the
Yalu concessions and by the unfortunate
war, and to plan the Counter-Revolution. . . .

" The delegates of this *Boïevaïa Droujina*
of cut-throats, or centurions (*sotniki*), as they
call themselves, met at St Petersburg at the
beginning of October. They were detained
in the city owing to the unexpected railway
strike, which prevented them from going
immediately to the scenes of their future
activity with the *mot d'ordre*, 'For the Tsar,'

---

[1] All prefects and governors of towns where massacres took
place.

to which was to be added according to circumstances 'Death to the Jews,' 'Death to the
students,' 'Death to the Intellectuals, to the
doctors, to the members of zemstvos, and even
to children.' It will therefore be seen that the
blood baths had been thought of much earlier
and for a totally different object, than the
one that took place after the manifesto of the
17th = 30th October. In some towns, indeed,
the patriotic zeal of the 'loyal' authorities
had already been manifested as they had lost
patience and the hope of seeing the return of
the centurions. Here, in St Petersburg, there
was anxiety on their account. An accident
gave the sinister old man the means of executing his devilish plan. On the 27th October
the strikers permitted a hospital train full of
patients to start for St Petersburg from
Moscow. The police took advantage of this
train [1] to send immediately by it on its return
to Moscow the centurions whom it had itself
helped to organise. They arrived on the 30th,
and at once stimulated and generalised scenes
of bloodshed, either personally or by telegraph,
with the *mot d'ordre*, 'For the Tsar,' to which
they added other incendiary cries according
to circumstances and the inspiration of the
moment. The country was inundated with
appeals to massacre its enemies ; such as Jews,
revolutionists, etc. Black bands were openly

---

[1] There are witnesses who intercepted telephonic messages on
this subject between General Bogdanovitch and the police.

organised with committees, sub-committees, and
patriotic and religious banners. There was no
longer any restraint for 'agents provocateurs,'
'publicists,' and preachers. At the same time
thirty-five regiments of Cossacks were let
loose on Russia, and seven million roubles
were expended.

"And all this ignominy, all this shame and
horror, of which all the governors and their
staffs, all the prefects of police and the whole
of the gendarmerie had been informed, did
not receive a word of countermand at the
moment of the proclamation of liberty! The
internal enemies remained the internal enemies.
It was on a secret order from St Petersburg
that the epidemic of bloodshed spread over
the whole of Russia. And when 'success'
exceeded the boldest anticipations, the whole
blame was laid on the people. 'You see the
population itself has taken part in the horrors;
children were torn to pieces or burnt alive,
women's bodies were split open and filled
with wool . . . they are barbarians, savages,
bashibazouks. What freedom can be given
to such people? They must be held in leash,
and in addition to that, starved and kept in
order by means of the whip. It is shameful
to be a Russian after that! Let us go abroad!
(During one single week, from the 13th to the
19th November, 26,000 foreign passports were
made out.) But stay, we will have another
little blood - letting, by splitting another

100,000 bodies.' Thus a counter-revolution was prepared, and it turned out a counter-constitution."

The author describes in indignant terms what happened in Russia after the 31st October: the fresh perjury of the Tsar, who after having promised freedom delivered Russia over to the Cossacks and to the black bands, the reign of duplicity and anarchy under Witte, etc. He makes a despairing appeal to the Government to establish at last the reign of liberty and of right, which alone can pacify and unite the country: " If not, we shall go back into the arms of the Revolution, to the bondage of the Prussians, to annihilation, and this will be the end of the country."

Thus the organisation of the massacres was revealed.[1] The greater number of the names connected with it, such as Kleigels (St Petersburg, Kieff), Neidhardt (Odessa), Moedem (Moscow), Deduline (St Petersburg), Sleptzoff (Nijni - Novgorod, Tver), Stolypin (Saratoff), Piler-Pilchau (Rostoff), Kurloff (Kursk - Minsk), Chirinkine (Baku),

[1] See Appendix.

etc., are known to my readers, as the European papers and ourselves in the course of our campaigns have quoted them over and over again. I will therefore only say a few words on the commander - in - chief of the black bands, General Bogdanovitch, the friend of Nicholas II.

This old man is famous in Russia for having instituted a patriotic organisation which publishes and distributes reactionary pamphlets by which Tsardom is glorified. His orthodoxy is uncompromising, but it cannot be said that his integrity is absolute, the friendship of the Tsar and his advisers having permitted him openly to commit acts verging on fraud. Before he organised the massacres, he became notorious by selling at exaggerated prices (as was admitted by his own son-in-law, General Petroff) snuff-boxes which he knew how to obtain from the Tsar, and by blackmailing Jews who were threatened with expulsion. For example, one Jew, the manager of one of the greatest sugar concerns in Russia, was suddenly expelled from Moscow under the Grand Duke Sergius. He appealed to General

Bogdanovitch, known as "the saviour of the rich" under such circumstances. The expelled man obtained the help of the General at a price of fifteen thousand roubles. The expulsion was, however, only postponed, so that the operation might be resumed at an early date. When the man brought the fifteen thousand roubles, General Bogdanovitch, looking as if he did not see them, said to the victim : " My friend, my wife, who thinks of all such details, has not forgotten that you have also promised her a hundred sacks of castor sugar. Well, do not forget them." It is all in keeping that this General should be at the head of the cut-throats, having as his agent General Trepoff,[1] the hero of the speech which has become historic, made by Prince Urussoff before the Duma on the day following the bloodshed of Bielostok.

[1] General Trepoff died since these lines were written — on 15th September.

CHAPTER VII

IN order to establish thoroughly the responsibility of the Government, I must give the text of a few of the indignant protests and warnings directed against the pogroms:

I

Proclamation of the Union of Unions[1]

The following proclamation was addressed "To all the citizens of St Petersburg" in connection with the massacres:

"In these days when the Russian people, after long efforts, have at last obtained the recognition of their rights, when a new order, more free and more just, has been promised

---

[1] An organisation representing the union of all professions on the basis of a general adhesion to the movement in favour of freedom.

them, men arise who, by means of lies and calumnies, endeavour to turn them against their own welfare. In this capital, leaflets are distributed which encourage the massacre of Jews and their friends. Here it is scarcely necessary to speak of this. We are convinced that the population of St Petersburg is not so unenlightened or so ignorant as to approve of such ignominies.

"But in many Russian towns these manœuvres have caused painful scenes of bloodshed. The first days of the new *régime* should have been a luminous festival of victory for the whole of the people, but these very days were darkened by cowardly and brutal excesses, by unheard-of violence practised on thousands of men. The cut-throats attacked even defenceless women and children. The Jews in particular have suffered. On the very day of the promulgation of the Manifesto, the streets of many towns were flooded with the innocent blood of these victims.

"How could such things be ?

"It is worth while to reflect upon it.

"Can it be that the Russian people do not desire liberty ? The more enlightened work-men and the whole of the 'intellectuals,' such as students, professors, lawyers, physicians, members of zemstvos, authors, etc., fight for the rights of the people.

"This is what they say : 'The people themselves must, through their representatives, take part in the government of the country and in the ordering of their lives. Speech and press must be free, so as to shed everywhere and at all times the light of truth and expose iniquity. The people should have the right of meeting in order to discuss their needs, and of associating in order to defend their interests.'

"These men, the pioneers, insisted and still insist on such rights belonging to the whole of the people. They ask that all classes of the population shall take part in the government and in legislation through their elected representatives, and that there shall be more representatives of peasants and workmen than of the wealthy classes—in proportion as the workers are more numerous than the rich. This would be a free government similar to that which has long been introduced into all civilised countries.

"For such a form of government all the foremost men among all the races of Russia—Russians, Jews, Esthonians, Armenians, etc.—long. With one accord they desire to live as the free children of a single mother—Russia. They desire a state of things which will be just and equal for all. These are the men who are called 'judaisers' by scurrilous prints. These are the very men who were robbed and massacred in Odessa, Rostoff, Kieff, and other towns.

L

"Who massacred them? Was it the Russian people?

"The defenders of the old *régime* say that it was, asserting at the same time that the people do not want liberty, that they do not want a new political system.

"The *tchinovniks* (government officials), the police and their hangers-on, have a reason for defending the ancient order of things and for fearing a new one. They feel that the end of their reign is coming, that they will not remain the masters, that they will not be able to enrich themselves by levying blackmail. Under the new system they will be controlled by the people, who will compel them to obey the law.

"For them the old times were really good times, and they would bring them back. They endeavour to persuade everybody that the people do not want to give up their old life either, that they know nothing better than the arbitrariness of the government officials and the police.

"We declare loudly that this is a lie.

"It is not the people who rise against liberty, against their best friends who are leading them to freedom. It is not in the interests of the people that the unfortunate Jews are massacred. They are cheats who, in their own pecuniary interests, and to save the old *régime*, spread all sorts of absurd stories about the Jews, and pretend that

they are the enemies of the Russian people.
The Jews as a people are as peaceful and
industrious as the Russians.

"'All men are brothers,' says the Gospel.

"'Death to the Jews!' cry the fanatics and
those in the pay of the police. But the
people do not hear them, only bands of men
who come from no one knows where, souls
which have bartered themselves away, and have
been paid for by the police. These outlaws
who have thus sold themselves, deliver the
cause of the people into the hands of the
nation's enemies.

"The unfortunate victims of the pogroms
are martyrs; they have suffered for the new
faith, for their faith in the liberty and happiness of the people. May the blood of these
martyrs be on the heads of the cut-throats!
Every honest man, if some coward is guilty
of violence, must render help to the victim
of such violence. All the leaders of the
pogroms, all the instigators and guilty ones,
should be called upon to render an account
of their misdeeds; all the fratricides should be
delivered over to justice.

"The Union of Unions, a league formed
by men of all classes and professions, declares
that it has already entered upon an enquiry
with regard to the persons who have taken
part in the pogroms, and that a list of the
guilty ones has been drawn up to be submitted to the courts."

II

Appeal of the Union of Russian Authors to Russian Society

" New Jewish massacres are being prepared in the south and the west of Russia.

" There are sinister rumours that in many towns the local authorities, the gendarmes, and the so-called 'true Russians' are making ready to lead ignorant men against the mass of Jewish inhabitants, deprived of rights and of means of defence. Pogroms are being organised, and carefully prepared in cold blood. Experienced and practised 'agents provocateurs' are busy with the sombre scenario.

" This is not the outcome of an over-excited imagination; it is an event of the day which is in process of becoming the terror of the near future—of the Easter holidays perhaps, that most joyful festival of Christendom, which is always chosen by evil-doers for the organisation of Jewish massacres.

" We repeat, our fears are not vain : all the world remembers the pogroms of Kishineff, of Odessa, of Gomel, and those very numerous outbreaks of last October and November, in which the participation of the authorities was so clearly proved.

"The names of Plehve and Neidhardt, of the gendarmes at Melitopol and at Kertch, of Count Podgoritchani-Petrovitch at Gomel, and of a multitude of small and great agents of the Government, are for ever identified with the organisation of Jewish massacres. This shameful association was proved with certainty by lawsuits which came before the courts, and even by enquiries of the administrative authorities, and by authentic documents deposited at the Ministry of Justice, as, for instance, in the affair of Kertch. It is, moreover, obvious to everybody. It is known to the whole world, and, above all, to those who deny it.

"We will not now speak of the steps taken in the past to prepare Jewish massacres. We have not the heart to repeat here what has happened in connection with these numerous St Bartholomews organised by the agents of the administration, with the help of all the refuse of society. This is known to everybody, and especially to those under whose auspices women were violated and nails driven into the heads of Jews.

"We will only speak of the present hour, and of what is being prepared for the future.

"At St Petersburg, in the official printing establishment of the Gradonatchalnik (prefect of the town), with the authority of the Censor, a proclamation has been printed recommending the killing and torturing of Jews. This proclamation is publicly and openly sold at the bookstalls of the *Novoïe Vremya*, and thousands of copies have been sent to the provinces.

" In Odessa, in the printing office of the General Staff of the military district of Odessa, an appeal of the same description but addressed to the soldiers has been printed. The Jews are described in it as the chief authors of our reverses in the Far East. The troubles at home are also represented by this appeal as being the work of persons in the pay of the Jews. It ends with an invitation to suppress this new Jewish enemy, and to boldly attack it.

" At Ekaterinoslav, in Christian circles, numerous copies of a pamphlet by a certain Kaloujsky, entitled ' Good Advice to the Jews,' are to be found. This pamphlet also is printed in St Petersburg, in the printing office of the Gradonatchalnik, and has likewise been approved by the Censor. It is little more than one long criminal calumny against the Jews, who, according to the author, should be exterminated at any cost. The ' good advice' to the Jews amounts to urging them to leave the country as soon as they can; if they do not, their fate will be what it was in Spain during the Middle Ages.

" The above information—for which we are indebted to the printing offices of the Gradonatchalnik of St Petersburg and the General Staff of the military district of Odessa, suffices to prove that the pogroms are carefully prepared, and to reveal the quarters where such preparations are made. According to absolutely reliable information, similar preparations have been made at Alexandrovsk, Minsk, Brest-Litofsk, Rostoff-on-the-Don, Krementchug, and many other towns and hamlets, whilst the press, controlled by the cut-throats of St Petersburg, is already spreading false rumours of a similar character. For instance, the blackmailing organ, *Degn* (The Day), writes: 'Take care of your children: the Jewish Feast of Passover is drawing near!'

"Yes, the Jews know what is in store for them, and they are leaving the country, leaving behind their hearths, homes, and property. They are emigrating from the whole of southern Russia to America, to Africa, to Australia, abandoning everything to save their lives, to be as far away as possible from the scene of the horrible crimes that are being prepared. And those who have no money for the journey! Obviously they are bound to remain behind. They remain and wait.

"Yes, the pogroms are being prepared, are almost ready. The lists are drawn up, the passwords made known, and a red mist of words, instinct with hatred and lies, reaches the muddled brains of the uncultured folk.

"We Russian authors, we address ourselves to Russian society. Shall we always remain indifferent spectators of the crimes which are covering us all with opprobrium ? Shall the perpetrators of the Jewish pogroms continue to make their preparations openly, insolently, before the whole world ? Amongst all the races oppressed by Russia's political power, there is not one whose history records as many savage and bloody reprisals as that of the Jewish people. Amongst all the Russian citizens who are subjected to the violence and arbitrary proceedings of the Russian Government, the Russian Jew stands alone, deprived of all rights, of all civic means of defence. We know how the Armenians were slaughtered in the Caucasus ; we have heard of the massacres of the students, which finally extended to the very schoolboys ;[1] we know the revolting savagery with which the Government treats the 'intellectuals' and all those who fight for freedom ; but in the Jewish question, in this nightmare of bloodshed which continually oppresses the whole of Jewry, we find concentrated as in a focus, and yet with striking particulars, Russian violence and the characteristic Russian denial of rights, all the horror and all the shamefulness of Russian life.

" The Jews are Russian citizens. The extermination of Jews is our own extermination ; it is the disgrace of Russia. The fight for the rights of the Jews which are trodden

[1] See the *Official Bulletin* of the Society of the Friends of the Russian people : "The Massacres of Kursk."

underfoot is a fight for Russian rights trodden underfoot; the emancipation of the Jews is our own emancipation.

"Russian literature—that part of it which is worthy of bearing the name, which cannot be bought and does not sell itself—only knows man independently of his creed and of his nationality. It has borne the pain of the whole of Russia, it has fought for the rights of all men. And at the present moment, when savage threats and sinister appeals are in the air, when we hear the groans proceeding from Jewish homes, and when provocation is once more endeavouring to bring about fresh bloodshed on Russian soil, which has already witnessed so many horrors, we Russian authors can no longer remain indifferent spectators.

"We appeal to you, Russian citizens, in the name of truth, in the name of conscience, in the name of your own honour and dignity. You, who love Russia, who are sincere and honest men, do not suffer the Jewish pogroms to be perpetrated, defend the Jews, put an end to the horrors of the Middle Ages! Let your indignation find expression in the municipalities, at public meetings, in the columns of the newspapers, in the streets and in public places. Send to the pillory all the instigators, all the accomplices of this iniquitous work! Take all steps which your honour and your conscience must inspire.

THE UNION OF RUSSIAN AUTHORS."

M

Simultaneously with the issue of this appeal, the scandalous acquittal by the Senate of Governor Kurloff, of Minsk, and of Prefect Neidhardt, of Odessa, was published by the Russian papers. Both these men were organisers, the former of the massacre of children at Kursk, and of "intellectuals," Jews, and workmen at Minsk—the latter of revolting slaughter at Odessa. The scandal of this acquittal of the 27th March 1906, consists in the defence of the cut-throats by the Minister of the Interior, Durnovo, in person, who declared that men such as Kurloff and Neidhardt could not and should never be held legally responsible, for in their actions they adapted themselves to the views and desires of the Government, and had been its faithful mouthpieces.

M. Durnovo thus confirmed officially what all the world knew, that the massacres had been organised, and are so still, by the direct agents of the Ministry of the Interior, by such men as Ratchkofsky (a friend of M. Delcassé); Launitz, formerly Governor of Tamboff, and at present Prefect of St Petersburg; his co-worker Bogdanovitch, the soul and inspiration of the bloody conspiracy of October; Count Kotzebue-Pillar-Pilhau, Prefect of Rostoff-on-the-Don; Sleptzoff, Governor of Tver; Podgoritchani-Petrovitch, of Gomel, who placed at the disposal of the black bands the printing office belonging to the revolutionists which he seized, etc., etc. (See speech of M. Vinaver at the Duma.)[1]

The organisers of fresh massacres, which the populations of the west and south await in fear and trembling, are thus sure of impunity, of encouragement, and of promotion.

The letters and the distressed appeals we receive from the unfortunate victims, exposed to the savage fury of the cut-throats, in which they implore us to appeal to the public opinion of the civilised countries, make the blood run cold. Amongst all civilised countries, England was the only one to intervene when the official news of the proclamation, which our readers will find later on, reached London. The Committee of the Russo-Jewish Fund appealed to the Secretary of State for Foreign Affairs, asking him to intervene in favour of the threatened

[1] See chap. xi.

population. The Foreign Secretary replied that he had already instructed the British representative in St Petersburg to draw the attention of the Russian Government to the danger, and it is noteworthy that the *Russian Government acknowledged the accuracy of the facts submitted to it, and promised to do all in its power to prevent the pogrom* by the dismissal of State Councillor Lavroff, who was chiefly responsible for the incendiary proclamation printed at the Ministry. But Durnovo himself, and General Bogdanovitch, who directs the "pogrom" organisation with the help of Durnovo, Launitz, and Ratchkofsky, chief police spy, all the real organisers of the massacres, went free, and are still working with impunity and unhampered at their task of shedding blood. They were thus all encouraged to prepare fresh pogroms on the first possible occasion.

The independent press of western countries, even of France, with *L'Humanité, L'Européen, Le Soir, La Tribune Russe, La Russie Libre, L'Aurore, La Correspondance Russe, L'Action*, etc., multiplied their warnings and protests.

Here is an example of what appeared last
May in the *Russie Libre*:

" The press has revealed the semi-official
steps taken by the English Government with
regard to the Russian Government, in view
of the pogroms which the agents of the
Government prepared all over Russia with
the help of sections of the notorious Union
of True Russians. The same steps have been
taken by the American bankers whom Witte
received at Portsmouth. Mr Krause, indeed,
wrote in their name a comminatory letter to
M. Witte, who replied that the Russian
Government would do all in its power to
prevent the renewal of massacres. As a
result of these steps, and especially in consideration of the necessity of reaching the
26th of April (date of the public subscription
to the famous Loan) 'without embarrassment
or accident,' we were spared massacres of Jews
at Easter. But, according to the information
which reaches us, they are only postponed.
The preparations of the cut-throats are not
abandoned. Their chiefs are all on the spot,
the fatal lists are drawn up, and the Cossacks
and the police are keeping in good practice.

" There is a rumour that the Government
hopes to provoke a fresh revolutionary outbreak by a whole series of illegal proceedings,
to which the Duma is to be subjected; if the
outbreak thus to be provoked does not take

place, there will be an anti-Jewish propaganda in order to supply the Government with the necessary pretext for fresh blood-lettings of Jews, 'intellectuals,' and workmen. It is in view of such massacres that all the famous cut-throats are not only secure in spite of official enquiries and reports which establish their guilt, but are provided with prominent posts and situations in which they can continue to serve in the same manner — their own manner — the savage bureaucracy of dying Tsardom.

"The day when these blood-lettings, which at the present time are being continued in the Caucasus and in certain Russian villages,[1] recommence in the cities and in the miserable Jewish Pale, we will tell the French public, the French bankers, and particularly the French Government, which, alone with the Turkish Government and that of William II., has not done its duty as a government of a civilised country: 'This is your work—a criminal work.' For the sake of support at Algeciras, which was more apparent than real, for the sake of the fallacious promises of a

[1] See telegram published in the Moscow papers of the 25th April: "Village of Kibarchino, District of Suraj, Government of Tchernigoff. On account of a little timber cut on the property of the Lord of the Manor and in consequence of troubles in a distillery, a punitive detachment was summoned, and carried out a pitiless and inhuman execution: five houses, six mills, and a shed were burnt down. Two peasants were killed, several mutilated, and all without exception flogged."

Witte, and particularly for the commission
of a hundred and twenty millions which the
bankers gained on the Loan of the 26th of
April, you sold to the assassins and the bandits
of Tsardom a hundred and thirty millions of
human beings, you compromised the work of
liberation which the Russian people and the
allied peoples are carrying on. You have
supplied the sinews of war to the greatest
enemies of Russia and of civilisation. We
shall never forget the silence of the French
Government. We shall never forget that
Loan directed against Russia and against
humanity."

On the 5th December last the Paris
Committee of Protest against the Massacres
published the following appeal, which had
previously been handed to the chiefs of all
the Parliamentary groups in the Chamber
of Deputies :

"*An Appeal to Europe*

"Paris, 4*th December* 1905.

" Sir, — The inhabitants of several large
towns of Russia such as Nikolaïeff, Odessa,
etc., implore all civilised nations and their
respective governments to take all possible
steps in St Petersburg to prevent a catastrophe

which may exceed in horror all the events of
these later days. (*Cf.* Reuter's telegram, 4th
December.)

" We implore you, Sir, you and the members
of your group, to speak before it should be too
late.

" You have read to-day in the papers, that
General Kaulbars has resumed in Odessa the
manœuvres against the Jews which were so
horribly successful in the hands of his predecessor, the Prefect Neidhardt, who pointed
out the Jews to the black bands before letting
the latter loose on the unfortunate city on the
Black Sea.

" We do not insist, Sir, on the humanitarian
side of the question. We would only recall
to your mind the point urged by Professor
Seignobos on Friday, the 1st December last,
at the meeting in the Salle Cadet. What the
Professor said was approximately this : Certain
Deputies called the attention of the President
of the Council, M. Rouvier, to the desirability
of exercising friendly pressure on the Russian
Government, under the present serious circumstances which may have a disastrous effect on
the moral and material interests of France.
M. Rouvier recognised the gravity of the
situation, but urged that the taking of steps
by the French Government would be a more
than delicate matter, and might even be
dangerous, for a collapse in Russia might
cause in France, not only a financial collapse,

but also an industrial crisis, since many French financiers have their floating capital in Russian stocks. To this, however, Professor Seignobos replied that it is precisely because the present state of things is perilous to the interests of France that it is the duty of the French Government to intervene with friendly advice in order to obtain from its *friend and ally* the cessation of massacres, and the introduction of the reforms which have been promised since 30th October last, and which, once introduced, will put an end to the state of anarchy which oppresses Russia and the whole civilised world.

"It is not the policy of the ostrich, but that of broad daylight, and of liberality, which is most suitable for Republican France, and which alone can prevent a cataclysm, the like of which the world has not yet seen.

"It is our duty to draw your attention to this perilous state of things. We are confident that Republican France, who marches at the head of civilisation, will not forget its duty."

Who will say that there was no foundation for all those warnings, after reading the revelations of Prince Urussoff, Joint Minister of the Interior at the time, after recalling the massacres at Gomel in the month of January, and those that followed at Vologda, Bielostok, etc., etc ?

N

CHAPTER VIII

It has been established that the pogrom proclamations of the Monarchists, exciting the masses of the people against the "intellectuals" and the non-Russian populations, were printed in a clandestine printing press in the building of the political police department (Fontanka, No. 16), under the direction of the gendarmerie officer, Komissaroff, and the assistant Director of the Department, Ratchkovsky. Similar proclamations in the name of the Union of the Russian people, inciting to murder not only of private individuals, but also of Witte, the so-called author of the movement in favour of liberty, were printed by the press of the Prefect of St Petersburg. Called before the Council of Ministers to give explanations, the Prefect, Launitz, the ex - cut - throat of Tamboff, and Belgarde, the director of the

Press bureau, treated the matter with levity and nonchalance. The former said that the proclamations were printed because they were authorised by the censor, and the latter that the censor who had given the authority was a man not altogether devoid of merit. Durnovo, the Minister, kept a profound silence during these explanations. The two officials were not interfered with, and have kept their posts.

We give a literal translation of one of these official proclamations, which was sold at two copecks a copy in the offices of the *Novoïe Vremya* and the *Russkoïe Znaméa*. This is the proclamation which called forth the semi-official intervention of the British Government:

"*Appeal to the Russian People*

" The cause of all the misfortunes of Russia.

" Measures for suppressing the evils caused by Jews.

" Do you know, brethren, workmen, and peasants, who is the chief author of all our misfortunes? Do you know that the Jews of the whole world, inhabiting Russia, America,

Germany, and England, have entered into an alliance and decided to completely ruin Russia, to divide it into small kingdoms in order to give it to the enemies of the Russian people, to give to them our mother Russia, conquered by Russian blood and soaked with Russian sweat?

" They would then, by means of lies and craft, take away the land from the Russian peasant, make him the slave of the Jew, do away with our priests, and convert the Orthodox churches and monasteries into Jewish stables and pig-styes. The first thing they did to ruin Russia was to incite the Japanese against us. During the war they betrayed us at every step. They sold us to our enemies, and this was the cause of our unheard-of defeats. And now they have made up their minds to do away with the only defenders of the Russian people and of their faith—the Orthodox landed proprietors and the merchants and manufacturers—in order that the Jews may appropriate everything in Russia without anybody being able to take up the cause of the Russian people.

" Our enemies have at their disposal a great deal of money, a great many millions for carrying on their miscreant work. And it is not only the Jews and other people of non-Russian origin who detest Russia, but also many Russians and dishonest Poles, who have lost their God and their honour, and contribute to the loss of our beloved and unfortunate country, some for the sake of filthy lucre, others from folly. All these vile miscreants, for whom the very gallows is not sufficient, pose as friends of the people, smuggle themselves into factories and villages, and take advantage of your ignorance and trustfulness, deceive you by specious promises, and incite you to all sorts of strikes of factory workers, railway officials, postmen, and others, as well as to pillage and burn the houses of the landed proprietors and all their property.

" Learn, therefore, poor trustful people, that by obeying these cowardly agitators you will only dig for yourselves a pit : when you have ruined factories and workshops by strikes, and burnt and pillaged well-ordered properties— Russian properties with schools, hospitals, and all sorts of establishments which you your-selves need—the whole of our poor country will be transformed into miserable ruins. Then the Jews will transfer their money from England, America, and Germany to this country, and will repurchase for a mere song all our factories, workshops, and properties. Then, by treating you to drink in order to catch you in their nets (at which they are such experts), they will speedily get hold of all our land and make dumb slaves of you all.

" They will make you work night and day, and pay you just enough to keep you from dying of hunger. On the slightest resistance on your part they will put you in prison, and leave you to rot there for years without compunction. In the courts of law there will only be Jews and their mercenary Russian hangers - on whom they have bought, and, however just may be your cause, you will be condemned by these courts, since, in the eyes of the Jew, any Christian is worse than a dog, and since, with regard to Christians, he knows neither conscience, pity, nor justice.

"There will be no one to take your side, since your natural defenders, the Orthodox landowners, manufacturers, and merchants will have been ruined by yourselves, and will have fallen into the clutches of, and will be dependent on, those same Jews who sold Christ. Brothers in Christ! Do not believe the honeyed words and the promises of the Jews and of their mercenary tools: they are not working for your good. These mercenaries are helping the Jews to ruin Russia, helping them to buy this ruined country for a mere song, and to found in it a Jewish kingdom.

"Whenever those betrayers of Christ come near you, tear them to pieces, kill them. At the present time all honest Russians, those who love Russia, are endeavouring to induce the Emperor to dismiss as soon as possible from his post as Prime Minister the principal enemy of the Russian people, the principal collaborator of the Jews, with his Jewish wife. God grant that the prayers of Russia may be heard ! At present the order is given to elect to the Duma representatives who will approach the Tsar in connection with your affairs.

" You must therefore endeavour to elect peasants who are not drunkards, who believe firmly in God, and who are honest. All your happiness and your future welfare depend upon this.

" Therefore save yourselves, Russians and other people inhabiting Russia, and loving your country, save yourselves from perdition.

" Time is passing quickly, and the Jewish peril is approaching as quickly. If it is not put an end to, a moment may come when to fight will be impossible. Therefore, to prevent the evil deeds of the Jews from becoming more general, it is necessary to take the following measures :

" 1. Expel all Jews without consideration of position or station in life, from all Russian towns in Europe and Asia, and locate them within the Jewish Pale, giving them one to five years to wind up their commercial and other business, according to orders given on special consultations instituted by governors and prefects.

" 2. Grant within the Pale the right of commerce, of work, and of trade to a limited number of Jews, in proportion to the number of the commercial and artisan class of the original population. Jews shall be prohibited from engaging in the corn, meat, and forest produce trades. They shall be absolutely prohibited from opening, managing, or taking part in brokerage, banking, financial and commercial businesses and similar institutions.

" 3. The rest of the Jewish population shall have the right to enter as workmen into the factories and into the employment of land-owners, and to engage in the work of masons, navvies, carpenters, etc.

" 4. It shall be left to the discretion of the governors to give leave of absence from the Pale to visit other parts of Russia (with the exception of the capitals, which Jews shall be completely prohibited from visiting) for a period not exceeding seven days, with the guarantee of a wealthy Jew. In the case of an absence, that is to say, of a stay outside the Pale of more than seven days, the guilty party shall be fined 300 roubles at least, and shall go to prison for from two to three months.

" 5. All Jewish schools shall be closed, and permission shall be given to the Jews to enter into Russian schools, in accordance with the general regulations.

" 6. Jews shall be deprived of the right of entering any superior, secondary or special educational establishment.

" 7. Jews shall be deprived of the right of having special butchers.

" 8. Jews shall be compelled to celebrate

their religious services on Saturdays and on
their holidays under the same conditions as
persons belonging to any other sect.   In
general, Jews shall be deprived of any special
privileges, and shall conform to the general
laws of the State.   With regard to military
service, since it is not only useless but
dangerous to have defenders such as the
Jews, a law shall be enacted, according to
which, for each Jew who is liable to military
service, the whole Jewish population of Russia
shall be bound to pay a fixed sum.

"9. Jews shall be prohibited from acting
in any way as public or State contractors or
purveyors.   Jews or Russians guilty of having
acted as such contractors or purveyors under
fictitious names, shall be liable to a term of
imprisonment of one year at the least.

"10. Public Rabbis shall be suppressed, and
their civil offices transferred to the town
authorities and to the municipal offices, or
performed by persons appointed by the
Government.

"11. In the event of the return of Jews
after their departure from Russia, they shall
be condemned to hard labour in prisons for a
year at least, and they shall then be located
for the rest of their lives in the district of
Kolymsk, government of Yakutsk (Eastern
Siberia).

"12. Jews shall be allowed to emigrate,
without right of return and of absence, to

o

the district of Verkhoyansk, government of Yakutsk, thirty acres of land being allotted to each of them free of charge.

"13. All Jews who have taken Russian or foreign names shall be compelled to substitute for such names within a year ancient Jewish names, and they shall be prohibited in future from taking fresh names, under a penalty of 300 roubles, and a term of imprisonment of from one to three months.

"14. Jews shall be prohibited not only in the whole of Russia, but also in their permanent places of residence, from accepting operatic or dramatic engagements at any theatre, under a penalty of 300 roubles in each case, to which Jews as well as the theatrical managers shall be liable.

"15. The governments of Kieff, Tauris, Kherson, and the towns of Ekaterinoslav and Kishineff shall be excluded from the territory reserved for the Jews.

"16. All persons of the Jewish faith without distinction of position, who may have acquired properties within the Pale of their residence, as well as outside such pale, shall be compelled to sell such property within a period of five years. If at the expiration of such period it is still unsold, it shall be disposed of by public auction.

"17. The population of the country and the towns, within the pale of residence of the Jews, shall be given the right to issue decrees of expulsion in cases of acknowledged rowdiness, by virtue of the law giving to rural communities the right of expelling from their midst members who are harmful to the community by reason of their conduct.

" 18. Foreign Jews shall not be given the right of naturalisation.

" 19. The publication of newspapers in the Jewish language shall be forbidden, and Jews shall be prohibited from acting as editors of any Russian papers whatsoever.

" 20. Jews in townships shall be subjected to the ordinary communal regulations.

" 21. Jews shall not have in their service Christian domestics or workmen.

" 22. Only young Jewish children embracing the Orthodox religion shall enjoy all rights given to the rest of the Russian population.

" In order to save Russia from her future peril and to execute the above measures, unshakeable firmness and a great deal of civic courage are required, also unfailing coolness, and the conviction that this is a sacred cause, involving the saving of the people from an ever-present internal enemy. This requires the genius of Peter I., the iron will of Nicholas I. and of Alexander III. ; it requires the decision with which Alexander II. entered upon the work of the emancipation of the serfs; it requires the iron will of Bismarck, and the political firmness of England during the war against the Boers, when the whole world was crying out against her. Hesitating and palliative measures towards the Jews can only create difficulties for those in power, and the acceleration of the revolution, for which all the Jewish 'intellectuals' are working. All organs of the Government must work conscientiously together, and act in a relentless and never-failing manner. The organs of the local administrations and of justice should work hand in hand; the laws concerning the Jews should be literally carried out, and all those who, from weakness or from lack of conscience, refrain from executing them, shall be punished severely as if for a political crime. Only when such measures against a common internal enemy shall be realised, will peace and calm be established in Russia.

" Let every Russian know that the whole strength of Russia lies in inviolable Autocracy and in Orthodoxy, and the names of the people who will at last have saved the Russian people from Jewry, and realised the aforesaid measures, will be inscribed in golden letters in the pages of history.

Authorised by the Censor.
ST PETERSBURG, 19*th February* (4*th March*) 1906.

" Printing press of the Gradonatchalink (prefect), Persp. Izmail, 8th line, No. 20. This publication is in stock in all the stores of the *Novoïe Vremya,* and in the editorial office of the *Russkoïe Znaméa*, St Petersburg, 4th line (rota), No. 6."

This proclamation, provided with marginal notes by Trepoff, should dispense with the necessity for further evidence ; but we will proceed.

CHAPTER IX

THE official organ of the party of the Liberty of the People, the *Retch*, published in its issue of the 9th May (26th April) the following document under the title " Contributions to the History of our Counter-Revolution. (Extract from an official report)."

" The Manifesto of the 17th (30th) October has been generally received with joy. The extreme parties denounced the utter discrepancy between the actual state of things in the country, and the great principles of political and civic freedom announced by the Manifesto, and the distrust with regard to the realisation by the Government of the promises given by the Manifesto. Unfortunately the population in the course of the past year considered itself over and over again entitled to complain of the lack of sincerity on the part of the Government and its promises. It was therefore natural that once more the people, while applauding the Manifesto on principle, only believed in the success of the fight for freedom in a few cases. The majority of the people adopted an expectant attitude, as they desired to see what would be the actual changes effected by the Manifesto. With regard to the extreme parties, they asserted as usual that the Government had no intention whatsoever of giving freedom to the people, and that the Manifesto was nothing but a political trick, to which the Government had resorted in view of the general strike, the stoppage of the traffic on all the railway lines, the insurrections in several of the large towns, and the growing unrest in the army.

"As we have said before, the agitation carried on by the extreme parties was at first only successful where the ground for disorder had been prepared, either by extremely oppressive economic conditions, or by the pressure exercised by the classes in power, or by unskilful or insincere acts of the administration. The extreme parties had gained in strength, chiefly because in their violent criticisms of the Government, they were mostly right. These parties would have lost all their prestige if the masses had seen, immediately after the proclamation of the Manifesto, that the Government really intended to pursue the new path they had indicated in the Manifesto, and that they had actually entered upon it. Unfortunately just the contrary took place, and the extreme parties had yet another opportunity—the gravity of which it is almost impossible to gauge—of boasting that they alone had been able to fathom the true worth of the promises of the Government.

" The very day of the proclamation of the Manifesto was marked by bloodshed in St Petersburg, notably by the shooting down of the crowd, which marched in a peaceful procession to the Gorokhovaïa and the Perspective Zagorodny. And after that blood was shed all over Russia. The number of the killed and seriously wounded during the four or five months which followed the proclamation of the Manifesto is difficult to ascertain; but according to absolutely reliable information it is estimated at some tens of thousands. But the worst of all was, that the population was firmly convinced that all these pogroms — which took place unexpectedly and simultaneously all over Russia, and drowned in blood the exultation caused by the liberty promised to the people—were provoked and carried out by one and the same hand, that of the authorities. Popular belief and the press asserted that the pogroms were the result of provocations by the Government for the purpose of preventing the carrying out of their own pledges. Unfortunately, the population had only too many reasons for thinking so. The local authorities as well as the superior authorities had from the very first adopted an unsympathetic, if not hostile, attitude towards the Manifesto.

" Major-General Debil thus expresses himself in a telegram sent from Lublin to the head of the corps of gendarmes on the 19th October (2nd November) : ' To-day, after the proclamation of the Manifesto of the 17th October, in view of the order given by the Catholic Bishop to celebrate masses in the churches, a service took place in the Cathedral.' Therefore, it was only because the Catholic Bishop took the initiative that the local authorities thought it improper not to do likewise on the occasion of such a remarkable act of grace from the monarch towards the people. But in the cases where the local authorities, even the most highly placed, suggested measures for ordering real life in accordance with the promises of the Manifesto, they met with uncompromising hostility from the superior authorities in St Petersburg. Thus, for instance, the temporary governor of Poland, Bekman, reported by telegraph to the Minister of the Interior as follows : ' The commander of the fortress of Libau telegraphs that yesterday a meeting of twenty thousand persons of an extreme and decisive character, sent him five delegates to explain to him their demands based on the Manifesto of the 17th October. (1) To abolish the state of siege and of reinforced protection ; (2) To recall the Cossacks and Dragoons ; (3) To

P

release immediately all political and administrative prisoners. In the event of these demands being granted, the delegates promised absolute quiet and the resumption of work : in the contrary case, the continuation of troubles, and of the strike. The commander requests instructions, and supports the demand for the abolition of the state of siege. For my part, I think that a state of siege no longer meets the present situation.' Therefore the commander of the fortress and the governor-general, that is to say, the persons directly responsible for the peace of the town, demanded the suppression of the state of siege. To this they received the following answer : ' In reply to your telegram of the 20th October, I do not agree with your conclusions with regard to the incompatibility of the state of siege with the present situation. Instructions follow shortly. Trepoff, Assistant Minister.' (Telegram in cipher of the 21st October, 2952.)

" The population, inspired by common-sense and generally well informed with regard to what was going on in the government institutions, could not but be troubled by the fact that a state of siege, acknowledged to be useless in itself, was allowed to continue only because in theory it was compatible with the existing state of things. Even before this it had had but little confidence in the Government. It was therefore naturally inclined to

believe that this compatibility consisted chiefly
in the fact that under a state of siege it was
easier not to carry out the liberties granted
to the people. Then, in a population which
on the previous day guaranteed complete
tranquillity in case the Government should
carry out its promises, commenced a movement of protest which was all the more
pronounced because the people no longer
fought for revolutionary principles, but for
strictly constitutional rights; because it no
longer strove for new liberties, but in defence
of those given by the Sovereign's Manifesto.
From that moment the population was convinced that it was on legal ground, and that
it was defending the prerogatives of imperial
power, whereas the Government was carrying
on a counter-revolution in order to take
from the people by illegal means the rights
which the Sovereign had granted to them.
The people were above all angered by the
fact that the fight was carried on by illegal
means, notably by brutal violence and
'pogroms' perpetrated by the dregs of the
population under the leadership of the police,
and with the knowledge and encouragement
of the higher authorities.

"Was this really what took place? The
question is so grave, and an affirmative answer
would leave such an indelible stain on the
honour of many men, that it is difficult to
reply to it; but in any event we may say that

the population, which judges the intentions of the authorities chiefly by their acts, had serious reasons for accusing them of having provoked and organised pogroms. According to the official version, the pogroms always took place in the following manner: A crowd of patriotic demonstrators followed the portrait of His Majesty the Emperor. This was shot at by a Jew. This infuriated the crowd, which immediately proceeded to pillage and massacre the Jews. During the first day the authorities proved powerless, and then in most cases, without a single blow, succeeded in dispersing the mob, and in restoring order.

" First of all, the people pointed out the strange uniformity of all that took place. It was always the crowd following the portrait of His Majesty — a proceeding which had never taken place before—there was always a Jew shooting at it, there was always the same revolver shot with identical results, including the powerlessness of the authorities to repress the pogroms, which were nevertheless carried on by a small band of men. And the population gave their own version of these pogroms, which on the face of it certainly supplied a better explanation of the uniformity of these occurrences. According to their version, the crowd of patriotic demonstrators consisted of the dregs of the population, of hooligans recruited by the police and frequently paid ; the shot which mostly hurt no one was fired by a police agent, and then the crowd, led by the police, commenced to sack and kill until given the signal to desist.

" In order to ascertain which of these two versions is the more correct one, we must examine the details. All the facts contained in the following statement are exclusively obtained from the documents of the Ministry of the Interior, and chiefly from those of the police department.

" 1. Did the higher government officials take part in the local organisation of their partisans ? There is every reason to give an affirmative reply to this question. In his confidential letter of the 1st September 1905, the Governor of Tula writes to Major - General D. F. Trepoff :

" ' Your Excellency will see from the enclosed letter that on the 2nd (15th) September a private consultation of well-intentioned persons will take place at Tula for the purpose of forming a union in the interests of the Government. I have no reason for not permitting such meetings, considering their object, as well as the persons of whom they consist, as I am convinced that these consultations are undertaken in the interests of a definite public object. But by authorising meetings in one case, and by forbidding them in another, the administration will naturally create discontent, and will give rise to an accusation of partiality towards certain parties, which the population

will imagine has some electoral object in view
of the convocation of the *Imperial Duma.*'

" On this letter D. F. Trepoff made the
following note :

" ' I do not share this point of view. The
Government is bound to uphold its friends,
and to discourage its enemies.'

" This attitude of the superior powers
was continued after the Manifesto of the
17th October.

" In his telegram of the 20th October, sent
from Mitau to D. F. Trepoff, Lieutenant-
General Bekman reports :

" ' I am at the same time making attempts to
effect a union between the moderate classes of
society, for the purpose of organised resistance
to the proceedings of the extreme elements.'

" But in the opinion of the population the
resistance to the extreme elements organised
on the 20th October could only take forms
which had not been foreseen in the Manifesto
of the 17th October. This is why, when
the pogroms took place, the population was
firmly convinced that there was a terrible premeditated organisation with definite objects,
that is to say, for carrying on the work of
sacking and killing peaceful citizens, as the
Governor of Tula had rightly foreseen.

" 2. How were these patriotic demonstrations brought about, and were there not peculi-
arities about them which gave rise to the
thought that they were prepared by the police

authorities? Most assuredly, yes. Major-
General Chrinikine informs Major - General
Trepoff by a telegram sent from Tiflis on
the 22nd October:
  "'On the 20th October, in the midst of the
party of patriotic workmen, the idea was
conceived of celebrating the granting of
political liberty by the Emperor. It was
decided that on the following day a service
should be held at the military cathedral, and
that a salute should be given to the Viceroy
in front of his palace. On the 21st October,
towards ten o'clock in the evening, a group
of railway workmen came from hearing Mass.
At the same time another group of patriots
from the opposite side of the town was going
to the military cathedral, where a solemn
service was held on the occasion of the Tsar's
birthday. These patriots were bearing the
national flag and singing the national anthem.
When the parade was over, this group, which
had increased to about a thousand persons,
started to the sound of music playing the
national anthem, whilst others were singing
it. The national flags were displayed, and
the portrait of the Emperor, on which were
written the words " Long live Freedom! " was
borne in front. Thus the crowd went towards
the Golovinsky Prospect, and then through
the Avenue Veriysky. In order to prevent
possible attempts at violence on the part of
the demonstrators belonging to the extreme

parties, the crowd was preceded by a detachment of dragoons, and followed by a detachment of infantry. All the time this procession lasted, the military band played the national anthem without interruption at the request of the demonstrators. At the barracks of the Corps of Cadets, the cadets and their inspectors came out, some of them joining the demonstrators. On the Mikhailowsky Prospect, close to the military college, the demonstrators met another crowd of railway workmen who were returning from early Mass at the Missionaries' Church. The pupils of the military college joined the demonstrators.'

"Thus at Tiflis there was already a 'party of patriotic workmen,' the demonstrations of which were under special protection. They were given a military escort and a military band, which obeyed the demands of the demonstrators. Cadets and pupils of the military college were officially authorised to join in these demonstrations. All this took place while demonstrations in the town were strictly prohibited and generally dispersed by troops, frequently not without victims. With exactly the same *mise en scène*, similar demonstrations took place in other towns, as, for instance, at Baku, as is shown by the following telegram in cipher, sent by Rear-Admiral Bal on the 21st October, No. 113, and addressed to the Admiralty :

" ' The demonstrators paraded the town accompanied by the band of the Caspian Fleet, and even entered the courtyards of the sailors' barracks, the portrait of His Imperial Majesty being borne in front, and the national anthem played. At that moment several sailors armed with guns came out of the barracks, attacked the crowd, and gave one workman a bayonet wound in his hand, but they were stopped by other sailors who were amongst the crews and in the procession. The sailors went back into the barracks with their guns. The commander of the crews had the gates guarded, and gave orders not to let anybody go out of the barracks. I immediately went to the barracks, and having been informed of what had occurred, I gave orders to surround the barracks with two companies of the Saliansky regiment. I then made them play the national anthem and shout ' Hurrah ! ' and suggested that the procession should continue on its way.'

" Thus, in their anxiety to organise patriotic demonstrations, they did not even stop before the danger of carrying away the army and the police, including the young cadets and pupils of the military college. The people, even those who had entirely kept away from politics, were perfectly aware of the danger of such manifestations for peaceful inhabitants. Thus the German Consul at Baku, Rell,

Q

telegraphed to the German Ambassador in St Petersburg on the 28th October :

" ' Quiet reigns at the present moment, but there is every reason for fearing that on Sunday the troubles will recommence, that there will be more incendiarism and bloodshed in the Armenian quarters of the town, where numerous foreigners reside. I would request you to make every effort that the local authorities should receive the strictest injunctions to do what they can in order to avoid any demonstrations.'

" This telegram was transmitted to the Ministry of the Interior, whence the following telegram was sent off to the Viceroy :

" ' The German Chargé d'Affaires requests that the persons and property of German subjects at Baku should be safeguarded. Do not fail to give the necessary orders.'

" The request of the German Consul not to permit demonstrations therefore proved unavailing.

" What, however, was much worse was that whilst the patriotic demonstrations were so much encouraged, all the others, however quiet they might be, were relentlessly dispersed. Thus Colonel Meier states in his cipher telegram sent to D. F. Trepoff from Warsaw on the 21st October :

" ' Demonstrations were to-day authorised in the case of crowds coming from churches bearing crosses, banners, and white flags of the Orthodox Church, and a few with Catholic priests. Crowds with red flags were dispersed.'

" Therefore the population could not fail to see, after the Manifesto of the 17th October, that patriotic demonstrations enjoyed every kind of protection from the authorities, whilst all other demonstrators were persecuted. The population also saw later on that these very participants in patriotic demonstrations perpetrated pillage and murder. *Unfortunately the conclusion was obvious, whether it was correct or not.*

" 3. Were all possible measures always taken to avoid pogroms? Unfortunately not in every case—very far from it. Nevertheless the population could not but think that such measures were necessary, against a crowd which sacked and killed peaceable citizens, whatever their political convictions might be. As an instance, we may cite the case of the ouprava (administrative council) of the Zemstvo of the government of Tver, whose building was burnt and the councillors and officials massacred by the crowd. The head of the gendarmerie of the government of Tver in his secret report to the Police Department of the 18th October 1905, No. 5317, gives the following account of this outrage:

" ' On the 17th October, about seven o'clock in the evening, in the ouprava of the Zemstvo of Tver, was held a private meeting of the officials to consider the question of their participating in the general strike. A group of about twenty - five persons looking like workmen tried to get in, but the porter did not permit them to enter. To their request that two delegates might be permitted to enter, some of the officials gave a negative reply, saying that persons not connected with the service of the administrative council were not admitted to the meeting, and they gave orders to lock the door. Some amongst the group began to strike against the door, and broke a glass pane, which provoked two revolver shots from the landing of the grand staircase. The group ran away from the door, throwing stones against the windows of the building. The police agents, reinforced by half a company of dragoons, drove away from the building the crowd which had gathered there. The Governor of Tver, who had arrived on the scene, admonished the crowd not to cause any troubles and to disperse, threatening them that he would have recourse to armed force against any who should disobey. In reply there were shouts: "They have met in the building to support the strike: arrest them, they are rebels. Sugar is already 25 copecks; they want to dethrone the Tsar, and have torn his portrait to pieces. We shall die for the Tsar." After having received assurances that

the guilty ones amongst the employés of
the administrative council should be punished,
the crowd dispersed, and mixed with the
public in the streets, amongst whom rumours
were rife that the assembled strikers had
fired on the people from the building, and
that there were some killed.   The crowd,
excited by this information, then rushed
towards the building, broke several windows
with stones, and, dividing into three parties,
started besieging the entrance to the administrative building, and the two entrances to
the courtyard.   The police force present
and the dragoons were powerless to restrain
the crowd, part of which, pushing aside the
agents guarding the gate, forced it open,
and, having invaded the courtyard, set fire
to the paper store belonging to the printing
press.   The fire caused a panic amongst
those assembled in the building, and they
rushed out into the streets from all the
exits, trying to lose themselves in the crowd
without being recognised.   About twenty-
five men and women were recognised and
beaten by the crowd, but without serious
consequences.   A fresh company of dragoons
which had arrived dispersed the crowd without any resistance on the part of the latter.'

" The population was bound to be im-
pressed by the patience of the Government,
which, seeing a crowd sack a public building,
confined itself to requesting that crowd not

to cause any commotion. Then the crowd, under the eyes of the troops and of the police, breaks windows, forces gates open, sets fire to the building. All this takes a long time, not less than an hour, but the troops and the police are there and take absolutely no steps, alleging as a reason that they are not sufficiently numerous. But it was obvious to every one that this was not an armed crowd of revolutionaries, but simply local hooligans, and a single volley was sufficient to disperse such a crowd, which departed without the slightest resistance as soon as it was ordered to do so. Unfortunately that order was not given until some persons had been killed and others seriously wounded.

" However, the same population knows perfectly well that in other cases the troops have fired on the crowd without orders. It is therefore fully convinced that the local authorities participate in the incendiarism and massacres.

" This conviction took root still more firmly owing to the circumstances of the Jewish pogroms at Kieff. As is shown by the secret report of the head of the Public Safety Organisation of Kieff, dated 31st October 1905, No. 3850, and sent to the head of the Police Department, the Kieff pogrom commenced on the 18th October. During the day only individual Jews were attacked, ' but at nightfall, as was to have been expected,

the populace began to sack the Jewish shops
in the Troïtzky and Jitny markets, and spent
its fury on innocent and unfortunate people.
The police forces and the troops dispersed
the crowd as far as possible, but it soon re-
assembled at other points, and sacked more
stores and shops. From many Jewish houses
revolver shots were fired on the mob, as well
as on the troops, especially in the neighbourhood of the Rue Vasikovskaïa, the troops
retaliating by volleys.'

" Therefore, according to absolutely reliable
information, the troops did not have recourse
to arms in order to disperse the mob. They
even sided with them by firing on those who
tried to defend themselves against that mob.
On the following day the same thing took
place on a still more extensive scale.

" ' From early morning in several parts of
the town there were seen crowds of workmen,
loafers, and ragamuffins, which commenced
attacking the stores and shops of the Jews.
Some members of this mob joined the patriotic
demonstrators. In a very short time it was
obvious that a pogrom was about to take
place. Crowds composed of several hundreds
of persons furiously attacked the Jewish shops,
breaking all they could find, and throwing
into the streets objects and goods on which
they trampled there and then, whilst other
persons who happened to be in the neighbourhood, chiefly peasants from the surrounding

villages who were taking no part in sacking the shops, picked up goods in the streets, and even took some from the stores themselves, carrying them away.

" ' The crowd invading the shops furiously tore up books, accounts, and correspondence, and broke large window panes of the shops, and objects of value. At the same time they did not touch any shops whose owners had exhibited images of saints or portraits of the Emperor at their windows and doors.'

" The efforts made by the troops and the police to prevent the pogrom did not avail, owing to the insufficiency of their number, the magnitude of the pogrom, and the activity of the mob. Only in a few places were the troops successful in protecting the property of the pillaged Jews.

" In some places a very apathetic attitude with regard to the pogrom was observed on the part of certain groups of soldiers and police where there were no officers. The Jewish shops situated in the Podol and Kretchchatik neighbourhoods, and in the Grand Vassilkovsky, suffered more than others through the pogrom.

" The result of the pogrom was the sack, in the district of Podol, of about a hundred shops, and the burning down of a whole row of shops in the Old Market. On that day about five hundred shops, stores, workshops, and Jewish apartments in all were sacked.

From Jewish flats in numerous houses shots were fired on the demonstrators, the murderers, and the peaceable citizens who were passing in the streets, as well as on the troops, the latter retaliating by volleys.

" Thus, according to the Chief of Police of Kieff, the troops and the police assumed an apathetic attitude towards the pogrom in various places. In general, no shots were fired at the mob, but recourse was invariably had to arms, and volleys were fired, as soon as any one tried to resist the mob. In these extraordinary circumstances the pogrom lasted two days, and the population became more and more convinced that the troops were only sent to support the mob.

" The sack lasted all day long, until a late hour of the night, and was then stopped by the troops, who commenced to disperse the mob with rifle fire.

" On the following day fresh serious attempts at a pogrom were made. At the Galitzky Market a crowd of more than ten thousand of the dregs of the population assembled, but the troops acted differently, and the pogrom did not take place. The population could therefore see that if the higher authorities wished, they could very easily stop the pogrom, and the natural conclusion was that if the authorities did not stop it, it was because they did not wish to do so.

" A few acts of the authorities in Odessa

K

finally gave the population the right to
directly accuse the Government of having
instigated the pogroms. In the night from
the 18th to the 19th October, the Prefect
Neidhardt caused the following appeal to the
population to be posted up in the streets of
the town :

"'In the name of the Prefect of Odessa.
I have before me a letter which a week ago
I showed to the head of the University, and
which is signed on behalf of the small tradesmen, peasants, and workmen. It is accompanied by an address worded as follows : "We
beg to inform Your Excellency that there are
internal disorders in the University. Is it
possible that the authorities of the University
who have sworn allegiance to our Little
Father the Tsar should have become the
chief amongst the revolutionary criminals,
and should incite dishonest young men to
meddle with affairs of the State? Has the
temple of science been founded by the State
in order that revolutionaries may meet in it,
stir up the people against the Government,
and no longer obey the legitimate require-
ments of that Government? It is an unheard-of thing that proclamations hostile to
the Government should be posted up in the
University, and that contempt should be
shown to the authorities by giving them
unseemly names. Our masters, servants of
the Tsar, have governed our state for a

thousand years, and now, in the opinion of a handful of semi-educated persons, they have suddenly become incapable of governing the people. It is shameful and injurious to see what the administrative power has allowed to occur. Your Excellency will forgive us if we express ourselves thus, but what can we do if the heart bleeds, and if it makes us wretched to see the arbitrary proceedings of our 'intellectual' rabble, which strives to deprive the Government of its power? We further take the liberty of informing Your Excellency, in the name of thirty thousand small tradesmen, that if Your Excellency does not take the energetic steps which our Little Father the Tsar has recommended you to take, we will go to the University and burn it down, so that our children should not learn to disobey the authorities. Why should the working classes meddle with these things? Do the authorities interfere with the working classes? On the contrary, the workman is happy when he is protected by the authorities. We urgently request Your Excellency to print this letter, and, in the event of your wishing to do so, to explain to our lower classes all that you may consider necessary. We also request you to send your explanation to all the churches, to our fathers (priests), who will preach sermons thereon." Here follow the signatures to the address. In drawing attention to this letter I would point out the

terrible danger with which we are threatened
in the case of a prolonged strike, and of the
increase of prices of food stuffs. At the
University, to which self-government has been
granted, but not the right of meetings for
outsiders, the meetings were accompanied by
unauthorised and revolting collections for the
purpose of arming the fighters. I pointed out
to the head of the University the inadmissi-
bility of such collections, which were bound
to lead to bloodshed, but neither the head
nor the council of the University took any
measures for the cessation of these collections
of money for the purpose of providing arms.
On the 12th October the pupils of the commercial school and of the Faïg school struck,
and nobody interfered with them, whilst they
themselves began to commit violences on the
14th October against the girls of the scholastic
establishments in the Kanatnaïa. The crowd
met a detachment of police agents number-
ing ten; when the policeman Soboleff was
wounded by a stone, the other police drew
their swords in accordance with the law. Two
grown-up young girls were wounded, and
one student, according to the enquiry of the
municipal administrative council, or six persons,
according to other information. After this
tales were spread in the town that the savage
police had massacred all the children of all
the scholastic institutions, and that one little
girl had been decapitated, and that at Mme.

Berezine's school all had been massacred without exception. All wise men should listen to such rumours with discrimination. There is a multitude of them abroad, each more terrible than the last. Yesterday, on the order of the strikers, all chemists' shops were closed from the early morning, and ambulances were established at certain selected spots, close to the intended barricades. Who had organised, foreseen, and prepared all this? Yesterday barricades were constructed in eleven places, the movements of the troops were impeded by displaced fences, by trees cut down, kiosks demolished, and the pavement torn up. More than fifty railway carriages were overturned. The troops fired several times, and, according to the hospital returns, more than eighty were killed and wounded. A crowd of young men sacked the armourers' store in De Ribas Street, carrying off all the weapons. The disorders and strikes have caused a terrible increase in the price of all necessaries of life. Whose fault is all this? Make up your minds on this point, wise men.

"'THE PREFECT NEIDHARDT.'

" This appeal contains an unmistakable and undisguised instigation of a certain part of the population against the University, against scholastic youth, and against the 'intellectuals.' Circulars of this description can provoke, and have since provoked, yet more terrible Jewish massacres.

" Thus the Prefect published a letter from thirty thousand small tradesmen, who threatened to burn down the University. Not a word has been said as to his considering such a measure illegal and inadmissible. In addition to this, he ends his appeal to the population by these words : ' The disorders and strikes have caused a terrible increase in the price of all necessaries of life. Whose fault is this ? Make up your minds on this point, wise men.'

" The population could not but regard this proclamation as an appeal for help to these ' wise men,' who were offering themselves to the Prefect in order to burn the University. When after this the pogrom took place, and the troops behaved as they did at Kieff, direct accusations were made against the Prefect in the town and by the press, and the Government was consequently held responsible for the bloodshed which took place on the days which followed.

" Thus these facts, obtained from the documents of the Police Department itself, furnish ample evidence that the greater part of the serious accusations brought by society and the people against the Government ever since the Manifesto, were based on absolutely valid reasons ; there were parties in existence which were created by the higher officials of the Government (local authorities) for the purpose of an organised resistance against the extreme elements. The Government organised patriotic manifestations and dispersed all others. Peaceable demonstrators were fired at, and under the very eyes of the police and the troops massacres of citizens and the burning down of a zemstvo building were permitted. The mob was not touched, and those who took the liberty of defending themselves were shot down by volleys. Intentionally or unintentionally, the crowd was incited to violence by official appeals signed by the higher representative of the Government in a large town, and when troubles resulted no measures were taken to repress them. All these events took place during a period of three to four days in different parts of Russia, and provoked such a storm of indignation amongst the population that the first joyful impression produced by the Manifesto of the 17th October was completely obliterated."

Did M. de Witte read this report, and did he mention it in his own report to the Tsar? This question is a damning one for M. de Witte. But we proceed.

CHAPTER X

(The Part played by Ratchkovsky and Timoféieff)

ALL doubts, if it were possible still to have any, vanish after reading the following document, also official, published by the *Retch* of 3rd May (16th) 1906 :

" To the Minister of the Interior from Councillor of State Makaroff, Director of the Special Division of the Police Department, delegated for special missions of the 5th class, and *attaché* to the Minister.

" *Report for* 15*th February* (28*th*) 1906

" On the receipt, on 11th February at the Special Division of Police, of the letter known to Your Excellency, and directed to the President of the Cabinet by the author

Obolensky on the subject of the massacres of Jews now being organised in the town of Alexandrovsk, in the Province of Ekaterinoslav, and with regard to the information which I communicated to Your Excellency on the 6th inst. concerning the drawing up, printing and issue by the Police Department of proclamations inciting the various sections of the populace against each other, I found myself wondering whether the massacres of Jews expected in the town of Alexandrovsk could not in very deed have been organised, as Obolensky asserts, by the officials, and whether the latter had not acted under the direction and with the cognisance of the police officials. Having examined the papers of the special division of the Ekaterinoslav police, I found amongst them two reports, addressed to the Department by the deputy of the Chief Superintendent of the Ekaterinoslav police force for the districts of Alexandrovsk and Pavlovsk, drawn up by Major Boudogovsky, dated 27th November and 5th December 1905, Nos. 1054 and 1061, which leave no shadow of doubt of the fact that the massacres of Jews in the town of Alexandrovsk were deliberately planned, that the unlawful disturbance created in furtherance of this object took place at the instigation of Major Boudogovsky, and that the police officials who were informed of it in good time, not only took no steps whatever to

ꙅ

suppress this agitation, but actually supported the action of Major Boudogovsky.

" To the above-mentioned reports of Major Boudogovsky were added six lithographed pamphlets and two printed ones, the latter with the stamp of 'The popular party of Alexandrovsk, October 17th.' The printed pamphlets are entitled, one 'To all True Russians, Citizens of Russia,' the other ' Is the Russian people in sympathy with Revolution and Republicanism?' and contain explanations to the people of the 'interested criminal' aims of the revolutionaries who are identified in the pamphlets with the Jews, and accounts of the events of 19th October last year, when a patriotic crowd in the town of Néjine compelled revolutionaries, students, and Jews to sing the national anthem, and to take an oath before the portrait of the Emperor.

" In their general style and by certain stray phrases, the pamphlets suggest methods by which one section of the populace might be inflamed against the other. One pamphlet printed in facsimile of handwriting contains a criticism of the public action of several members of the Zemstvo of the district of Alexandrovsk (mentioned by name in the pamphlet), using threatening expressions towards them.

" The other pamphlets in facsimile script, of which some are signed, ' Union of Russians

of Alexandrovsk, 17th October,' and one
'Russian Droujina (armed bands) of Alexandrovsk,' distinguish themselves by a particularly violent incitement of the people against
'revolutionaries, social-democrats, and Jews.'

"The first - mentioned are described as
brothers and slaves of 'Jews'; great stress is
laid upon the assertion that the revolutionary
movement is controlled entirely by Jews; they
close with the exclamations: 'Away with a
thought so devilish, so full of guile! Down
with the Jews and their social-democratic and
revolutionary colleagues! Down with the
Jews and their brother social-democrats and
revolutionaries!' As for the manifesto of
the Droujina of Alexandrovsk 'to all true
Russians,' it contains a savage demand for
the massacre of revolutionaries and Jews.
After having stated that Russia was being
dragged to perdition by social - democrats,
revolutionaries, and Jews, it continues:

"'Is it not enough for us that already at
St Petersburg the revolutionaries have usurped
the supreme power, and do not allow the
Tsar to promulgate the law in accordance
with the constitutional rights granted by him?
Even during the last few days this scum
of humanity, these social - democrats and
revolutionaries wounded the Tsar, Our Little
Father, whose hair has already been whitened
by grief. The German Emperor has despatched his battleships to St Petersburg.

As for us, true Russians, we shall perish if we do not band ourselves together in Droujinas and by our united efforts exterminate our enemy, the social-democrats and the Jews. It is not yet too late, but it soon will be, and the enemy that is in our midst will tear our beloved country into fragments and will deliver her up to be preyed upon by the Jews. Come then, bestir yourselves, rise up, you mighty Russian people, in revolt: form Droujinas, arm yourselves with scythes and pitchforks, and march to the defence of your Tsar, your Fatherland, and the Orthodox faith. But bear in mind that our foes are those very men who are so zealous for the present political strikes, who carry red flags and who call themselves social - democrats and revolutionaries. Therefore, true men of Russia, those of you who are for the Tsar, the country, and the Orthodox faith, come, on the first alarm, gather together with your arms, scythes, and pitchforks ready in your hands, and form up, near the public hall, under the tricolour flags of the Russian Droujina of Alexandrovsk which is well organised, and which, bearing with it the portrait of the Tsar and the sacred Ikon, will hurl itself upon those enemies of ours, the bearers of red flags.'

"In sending the said pamphlets to the Department of Police, Captain Boudogovsky, in his correspondence under the Nos. 1054 and 1061, states that these pamphlets are circulated by the 'Alexandrovsk Union of October 17th' in the town of Alexandrovsk and the adjacent villages, 'distributed in large numbers,' that they are 'of material utility in the work of combatting the insurrectionary movement,' 'that all the members of the said patriotic union were known to him, Captain Boudogovsky, and that he is employing all his influence in the distribution of similar pamphlets in the towns of his district also.' These, in his opinion, 'will have an excellent effect upon the peasantry, and will restrain them from acts of violence against the landowners.'

"Similar disclosures had previously reached the Police Department from Captain Boudogovsky, as appears from a marginal note made on one of his reports (No. 1054) by Piatnitzky, the *attaché* to the Special Mission Department, but I have not discovered these reports in the papers of the Special Division, although Piatnitzky, in presenting Captain Boudogovsky's Report No. 1054 to Ratchkovsky, director of the political agents of the Police Department, and Report No. 1061 to Timoféieff, chief of the Special Division of Police (at this time officer for Missions and *attaché* to Trepoff, the Governor of the Palace [1]) has made the following notes on the report:—On the first 'the appended manifestoes of the Alexandrovsk

---

[1] See *infra* the speeches of Prince Urussoff and M. Vinaver.

Union of 17th October bristle with inflammatory passages directed against the Jews,' and on the second, 'another series of anti-Semite pamphlets.' These reports did not result in any steps being taken in connection with the pamphlets by Councillor of State Timofeïeff or anybody else, but Captain Boudogovsky received his promotion.

" Concerning the author Obolensky's letter, addressed to Count Witte, Secretary of State, Your Excellency will be graciously pleased to notice that the agitation for the extermination of the Jews set in motion by the Alexandrovsk Union of 17th October at the instigation of Captain Boudogovsky, Deputy Superintendent of the Ekaterinoslav Gendarmerie, who acted with the tacit support of Ratchkovsky, the present Councillor of State, and Timofeïeff, has been crowned with success, and the massacre of the Jewish population of Alexandrovsk is expected to take place on the 19th inst. (4th March). Such acts as those of the above-mentioned officials, which lead to civil war and create favourable conditions for the increased development and success of the revolutionary propaganda, are crimes liable to punishment under Article 341 of the Penal Code. For this reason I consider it my duty to submit the foregoing to the judgment of Your Excellency."

This is the first time that in an official

report the responsibility is directly laid upon the shoulders of Ratchkovsky, the head of the political police and ex-chief of the Russian political police in Paris. He it was, then, who represented that gang of assassins-in-chief, Trepoff, Bogdanovitch, Durnovo, etc., in the very heart of the political police. "Who has restored Ratchkovsky to life?" asks the *Retch* — "Ratchkovsky, who broke his neck in Paris? At whose suggestion has this police spy been commanded to employ the troops and public organisation for the purpose of aiding the Government? Who is this Timoféïeff?[1] Whence has he come to St Petersburg? And finally, why has it not been possible, in spite of the wishes of its initiators, to proceed with the enquiry, commenced by Makaroff, cited in the official report which ended in the promotion of Timoféïeff and the Captain of the Gendarmerie himself? All the data necessary for answering these questions are in existence. The chain of evidence is complete." This chain of evidence leads to General Bogdanovitch, the intimate friend of the Tsar, and to Trepoff,

---

[1] See also M. Vinaver's speech.

who has restored Ratchkovsky to life ; Trepoff, who engineers pogroms, wielding vast power, at first secretly, but for nearly a year past in an official capacity by the will of the Tsar ; Trepoff, giving instructions to governors, chiefs of police, etc. ; Trepoff, who at this very hour reappears in the same part, at the same work, the tale of whose infamy has been handed down to posterity in Prince Urussoff's speech. The *Retch*, the official organ of the constitutional-democratic party, published in its issue of 18th May the following sinister paragraph :

" Rumour has it that on the advice of D. F. Trepoff it has been suggested (by whom ?) to the governors that they should urge the local branches of the loyalist party of the Union of True Russians, Monarchists, etc., to present an appeal from faithful subjects in which a request should be made that 'free pardons shall not be granted to criminals, and that the death penalty shall not be abolished.'"[1]

And, as a matter of fact, for some time past the societies mentioned have been sending in

[1] See chap. xiii.

petitions and appeals of this sort, and all of them are drawn up in the same terms and on the same model. At the same time we are informed that Vouitch having been appointed under the new administration in the room of the dismissed director of political police, Ratchkovsky has been attached to the new President of the Cabinet, and that massacres are being openly organised more or less after the same manner as those of last October, and that they have already commenced in several districts where the police and the agents of Messrs Trepoff, Ratchkovsky and Co. are more active.

Before citing the latest facts in proof of the responsibility of the high authorities in connection with the organisation of pogroms, it is interesting to note the political *début* of Ratchkovsky, who has played quite as important a part in previous pogroms as well as in the Gapon affair, and who is playing the same part in the pogroms which are now being organised. Like all the hirelings and spies of his breed, Zoubatoff, Manouïloff, etc., he at first pretended to be broad-minded, almost to the extent of revolutionarism, and was a

T

contributor to Liberal and even Judeophile
publications. Thus it is that we find in 1879,
in the first number of the *Narodnaïa Volia*,
the organ of the party of that name, the
following announcement of the Executive
Committee, dated 20th August 1879:

"The Executive Committee hereby an-
nounces that Piotrivanovitch Ratchkovsky,
Ex-examining Magistrate at Pinega, and at
the present time attached to the judicial
administration, contributor to the *Novosti*
and *Le Juif Russe* newspapers, is in the pay
of the Third Section.

"Description:—Tall, rather stout, black
hair and eyes, pale pink and white com-
plexion, large features, nose very big and
long; approximate age twenty-eight or
twenty-nine years. Thick black moustaches,
beard and whiskers at present shaved.

"The Executive Committee advises all to be
on their guard against this police spy."

This having been satisfactorily proved, let
us hear what the Duma has to say.

CHAPTER XI

THIS was the condition of affairs which led the Duma to challenge the Government as to the part played in the pogroms by the Department of Police.

Forty - seven Deputies, with the hearty approval of nearly all their colleagues, signed, and caused the Duma to adopt the following interpellation :

" Official documents have been published in the Press which clearly show that the Department of State Police was directly concerned in the mission of inflaming one section of the people against the other, a mission which has concentrated hordes of assassins in the midst of peaceable citizens.

" In particular, from the report of 15th February of the present year, made by Makaroff, Councillor of State, and published in No. 63 of the *Retch*, it seems to have been proved that the Police Department instituted a special printing office in which were printed reactionary proclamations, drawn up and distributed broadcast by the same Department, inciting the populace to massacre persons of other religions and the 'intellectuals.'

"This printing office was under the immediate control of Komissaroff, the officer of the Special Police Corps. In spite of the official enquiry, not only were no steps taken to prevent a similar unprecedented abuse of power in the future, but the individuals chiefly responsible were actually rewarded. For this reason, and because similar outrages have just been repeated at Vologda, Kaliazine and Tsarizyne, being convinced that they have taken place with the same criminal attitude on the part of the authorities, we request the Duma to approach the Minister of the Interior on the following points:

" Are the facts quoted above known to the Minister ? What measures does he propose to take for the punishment of the culprits, and what powers has he for the prevention of such crimes in the future ? " (Duma Report, 4th (17th) May 1906.)

The delay of a month provided for by the Constitution of the Duma having expired, M. Stolypin, Minister of the Interior, replied to the interpellation on 8th (21st) June. He

made a sort of half-confession, admitting the
existence of the secret printing office and the
action of the police under his predecessor, and
promising that during his term of office such
a thing should not recur.   With regard to the
"pogroms," he attempted to justify the conduct
of the police and gendarmerie at Vologda,
but was obliged to admit the abominable
nature of the conduct of the authorities at
Tsarizyne, etc.   He concluded, moreover, by
admitting his helplessness, and by asserting
that he was obliged to uphold bad laws until
new ones were made.   It was this pitiful confession which provoked the dramatic intervention of Prince Urussoff.

Prince Urussoff's Speech [1]

"Gentlemen and Representatives of the
People, I ask for a hearing, in order to draw
your attention to some points in the questions
put to the Ministry by the Duma, and in the

[1] The following commentary with which the account given of
the historic sitting of the Duma was accompanied in several of
the moderate newspapers, is not without interest:

"Prince Urussoff's stirring speech on the massacres of
October and of the present time is particularly interesting in
view of the following circumstances.   Under the Bouliguine

reply which we have just heard. I think that
we ought to examine the disclosures relating
to the printing machine which was hidden in
the inmost recesses of the Police Department,
and by which were printed the pamphlets
inciting the people to civil war, concerning

Ministry, a special police administration having been formed by
Trepoff, Prince Urussoff resigned the Governorship of Tver.
The reason for his decision was that he could not serve under
Trepoff, because Trepoff was responsible for the murder of the
Grand Duke Sergius, under whom he had been Chief of Police
at Moscow. It was not Sergius who deserved the bitter hatred
of the population of Moscow—hatred to which the Grand Duke
was sacrificed—but Trepoff, who had been astute enough to
screen himself. Fearing, therefore, that Trepoff's *régime* would
similarly and inevitably react upon the Tsar and have the
direst consequences, Prince Urussoff, as beseemed an official
devoted to the Emperor, handed in his resignation. Under
Witte, Prince Urussoff became Deputy Minister of the Interior.
A proclamation issued by the State Printing Press, and bearing
the Censor's stamp, then made its appearance under the title,
'Death to the Jews! Death to Witte, the Jewish Minister!'
Urussoff was commissioned by Witte to conduct an enquiry
into the matter. He discovered in the State Printing Office
printer's proofs bearing the written inscription, 'Passed for
printing, Trepoff.' He discovered also that the heads of the
provincial gendarmerie had addressed reports to St Petersburg
stating that, in accordance with the instructions sent from
St Petersburg, proclamations inciting the people to massacres
had been distributed, and that the desired effect upon the lower
orders had been obtained. Prince Urussoff, failing to obtain
authority to punish the culprits, again resigned. Now, as
deputy to the Duma, he has exposed what was the actual state of
affairs. In connection with these facts, it is worthy of note that
the military authorities at Bielostok declared to the Governor
and Radetzki, the Chief of Police, that they could not take
orders from the civil authorities to put a stop to the massacre,

ourselves not so much with the object of
determining the culprits responsible for what
has already been done, as with the disquiet-
ing possibility that the Government officials
secretly participated in the organisation of
those tragedies of bloodshed, which have
lately gained for them a shameful notoriety,
and which, as recent events show, continue
to provoke the indignation of all by whom
human life and the dignity of the Russian
Empire are still held dear.

"Let me explain myself. I do not doubt
for one moment the sincerity of the Minister
of the Interior, and it is not against the
Ministry that I shall direct my speech. This
is precisely where all the import, interest, and
gravity of the question under discussion lies,
namely, that the 'pogroms' and wholesale
butcheries will continue independently of the
attitude assumed by any individual Minister
of the Interior, or by any Ministry, because
the circumstances from which they arise are
permanent and find their origin in the sphere
of action of the Government. The declara-

as they had received orders, which they must obey, direct from
St Petersburg. This was absolutely illegal, since, according to
the Russian law, the civil authorities have, in time of internal
disturbances, the right in every case to instruct the military
authorities as to what they should do. We may add that Prince
Urussoff had been nominated Governor of Kishineff after the
first great massacres organised in 1903 by Plehve's subordinate,
Levendal, a Colonel of Gendarmerie, with the object of quieting
the population, a task in which he was successful."

tion of the Minister[1] in this respect did not strike me as being very forcible, and I will explain why. I shall have to touch in this connection on the question of 'pogroms,' and at the same time on the part played by the afore-mentioned printing office. The student of these so - called 'pogroms' is confronted with certain phenomena which are always the same.

"In the first place, the 'pogrom' is always preceded by rumours of its preparation, accompanied by pamphlets of an inflammatory nature, distributed amongst the people. These pamphlets are all worded in the same style, and put forward the same arguments. The dregs of the population, known only to the few, always make their appearance at such times, like birds of ill omen. Secondly, the officially announced pretext of the 'pogrom' given out at the very outset of the disturbances, invariably proves to be false.

"Further, in the details of the massacres we find a certain regularity which deprives them of any appearance of being accidental. The assassins do their work with a consciousness

---

[1] It contains gems of this kind : "Boudogovsky, Officer of Gendarmerie, organiser of the 'black hundreds' of Alexandrovsk, was at St Petersburg called upon for an explanation, but as the 'pogrom' had not taken place he could not legally be held responsible." "As for the rewards he received, these were for having restored order." The Ministerial defence of the Gendarme (Inspector Pychkine, who took a leading part in the Vologda and other massacres) was equally convincing.

of right and impunity, and only towards the
end does it seem as if they were not quite
so confident. The 'pogrom' is then quickly
and easily suppressed. Then again the action
of the police is never united, and whilst certain
quarters of a town are completely sacked, in
spite of large forces of police, others are left
almost entirely unmolested, thanks to the
vigilance of police agents, who perform their
duties with confidence and energy. Finally
the 'pogrom' is stopped, arrests are made,
and the authorities who visit the prisoners
cannot fail to observe that they have before
them not criminals, but merely ignorant men
whom some one has deceived.

"One is aware of the existence of a homo-
geneous and widespread organisation. Those
who call it a Government organisation deceive
themselves if they think that settles the question and clears up the matter. But they are
not completely deceived, and the events of
last winter, which led to our protests, will help
us to find our way in this fog which envelops
matters already hazy enough.

"In January 1906 an individual, occupying
a secondary post in the Ministry, but who
was known to oppose the policy of 'pogroms'[1]

[1] It appears from this that the policy of "pogroms" existed
while Durnovo was Minister of the Interior, independently of
the secret reign of Trepoff and Co. Moreover, the attitude of
Durnovo at the time of the Witte enquiry, and during the trial
of his murderous governors, as well as his declarations made to
Prince Oberliani, leave no doubt on the matter. We find, as a

—I am not referring to myself—began to receive in large quantities copies of pamphlets, neatly got up, which were widely distributed in the chief centres of the south and west of Russia. Fears and complaints were also expressed to him, announcing the preparation of 'pogroms' at Vilna, Bielostok, Kieff, Nikolaïeff, Alexandrovsk, and other towns.

"The Gomel 'pogrom' in January showed that the fears expressed had been well founded, and the individual in question was obliged to take all possible steps for the prevention of further 'pogroms.' He succeeded, thanks to the orders of the President of the Cabinet, who was kept informed of the progress of the secret enquiry, which threw some light on the

matter of fact, in the *Retch* (8th (21st) June 1906), the cynical and brutal declarations which the Minister of the Interior, Durnovo, made to Prince Oberliani, one of the chief members of the "Organisation of United Zemstvos," formed for the purpose of giving assistance to the peasants suffering through the famine.

I will pass over the brutal theories of this Durnovo, who has been publicly disgraced, even by moderate Monarchists like Stakhovitch, and who asserts that it is "immoral to feed the people," that he had arrested but a small number (80,000), that he wanted more, that the murderous governors had understood but a quarter of what he meant, but *if only one half had been understood, Russia would have been saved*. He added that he had in his service fools and intelligent men, men who know that there are two ways of serving : the one, doing less than they were asked to do ; the others doing more. In the first case he punished them ; in the second case he would give them all his support, as he has done in the case of Kurloff, Neidhardt, and other cut-throats.

gloomy scenes following the actions of the
'past masters in pogroms.'

" A number of persons forming the ' Droujina ' (armed bands) of one of our 'patriotic'
associations, and in league with persons who
were in close touch with the editorial manage-
ment of a newspaper, not published in St
Petersburg, undertook the struggle against
the Revolution.[1] In their character of
'patriots' and 'True Russians' they saw the
cause of the troubles in the Allogènes (the
inhabitants of the frontier provinces and of
the Jewish Pale of Settlement). Pamphlets
couched in violent terms and distributed in
tens of thousands of copies called upon the
Russian population, and particularly on the
Russian Army, to give no quarter to the
agitators. The members of this organisation
scattered pamphlets everywhere, and entrusted
them to other members and trusty friends,
who in their turn distributed them with discretion and intelligence. Strange and unfore-
seen consequences resulted with regard to the
unity of authority ; for instance, an assistant

[1] The *Moskovskya Vedomosti?* Here is a typical boast of the
" black bands": " We are no longer 'hundreds' (black hundreds
or black bands), we are millions."

Some days before the newspaper of the late Katkoff and his
successor assassin, Gringmouth, accepted with pride for itself
and its friends the title of "black bands," as well as the designa-
tion, "leader of patriotic massacres." For further particulars
of the part played by the *Moskovskya Vedomosti,* the *Novoïe
Vremya,* and the official organs, see chapter v.

prefect of police distributed proclamations
unknown to his superior; on the other hand,
every confidence was placed in the chief of
police in one district, while the chief of
the next district was distrusted. Special
sums were deposited with the officers of
the gendarmerie or of the detective force.
Suspicious-looking individuals began to visit
them, and rumours of certain preparations
were rife in the town. The terror-stricken
people went to see the governor, who
endeavoured to calm them, though he knew
full well that they were far from being safe.
The Ministry sent out despatches ordering
steps to be taken for the maintenance of
order and security, and the steps were taken,
but the instructions given did not always
inspire confidence. In many cases the police
spies honestly believed that those steps were
only taken to keep up appearances, while they
themselves were correctly interpreting the true
intentions of the Government. They read
between the lines, obeying, unknown to the
Government, a voice which came from afar,
and which inspired them with confidence. In
short, an incredible state of confusion was
produced, accompanied by utter demoralisation
and disorganisation of authority.

"During this time, at St Petersburg, since
the autumn of 1905 (before the formation, as
it afterwards appeared, of the Ministry of
October), a printing press was established in

a secluded room of the Department of the
Interior at No. 16 Fontanka, bought by the
Department with Treasury funds. A police
officer in plain clothes named Komissaroff
was attached to this printing office, and drew
up the proclamations with the help of several
of his creatures. The secret of this private
printing office was so well guarded, and the
doings of its organisers were so wrapped in
mystery, that few people knew anything about
it, not only in the Ministry, but even in the
Police Department itself. Meanwhile the propaganda of this organisation, of which the
aforesaid printing press was the instrument,
flourished exceedingly. Komissaroff, on being
questioned by some one who, quite by accident,
lighted on traces of his work, replied : ' We
are in a position to start a " pogrom," when
and how we please, with ten, or ten thousand,
men.'

" Gentlemen, this phrase has become historic.
(*Prolonged sensation amongst the deputies.*)
I may add for the information of the deputies
from Kieff that a ' pogrom ' of ten thousand
was fixed upon for 3rd February, but it was
successfully averted. (*Renewed commotion.*)
The President of the Cabinet was seized, they
say, with a violent fit of nervous asthma,
when he was told the facts which I have
just related to you. He sent for Komissaroff,
who gave him an account of his actions and
of his authority for them. A few hours later,

the printing press, the proclamations, and the
originators of the scheme had disappeared
from the Department. There remained only
an empty room. This is why no one, not
even the Ministry of the Interior, is able
to satisfy the legitimate desire of the Duma
to know the names of the ringleaders of this
organisation. Their impunity was guaranteed,
and a magic influence was exercised on the
police and other officials to procure even
rewards and promotion for the most energetic
amongst them. I cannot quote instances of
this, or other details of this affair, from
memory. I am speaking without preparation
or notes, and must of necessity leave much
unsaid. As it is, I have wearied you already.
(*Repeated cries of: 'Go on, go on!'*) It is
now time to draw the final conclusions from
all I have said.

"The first conclusion is this : The declaration of the Minister of the Interior gives us no
substantial guarantees with regard to definite
means of stopping the activity of those organisations which are engaged in planning wholesale
massacres, and in tempting State officials to
give their support to such butcheries. It is
easy to understand that as the chief promoters
and instigators are outside the authority of
the Ministry, it is a matter of indifference
to them whether the Minister of the Interior
preserves an attitude of benevolent neutrality
towards their doings, or whether he publicly

condemns them. I will undertake to say
that not even a Ministry drawn from the
Duma could restore order in the country so
long as these unknown wire-pullers are out
of reach, sheltered behind an insurmountable
wall, clinging with their grasping hands to the
different parts of the governmental machinery,
exercising their political ignorance by experi-
ments on living organisms, and engaging in
a sort of political vivisection. (*Loud and
prolonged applause.*)

"The second conclusion is still more melan-
choly, and concerns the Duma itself. Gentlemen, we who represent the people are gathered
here from the remotest parts of Russia, to
give utterance, not only to our indignation
and to our protests, but also to a burning
thirst for action, for sacrifice, and, in short,
for a pure and sincere patriotism. There are
among us many landowners who live on the
revenues of their property. Have you heard
a single one of them protest against the proposed compulsory dispossession in favour of the
hard-working tiller of the soil? Representatives of the privileged classes are numerous
among us. Have there been many objections
to the abolition of privileges, to the idea of
civil equality, and to reforms carried out in
the true democratic and popular spirit? Has
not even this 'revolutionary' Duma tried,
from the very first, to uplift the Imperial
diadem, to place it beyond the reach of

political quarrels, beyond the influence of
our mistakes and the responsibility for those
mistakes? One asks oneself if at the moment
of inevitable and urgently needed reforms
one has the right to demand any other Duma
than that in which private interests and class
differences have thus yielded to the triumph
of the national welfare. (*Unanimous and prolonged applause.*) Nevertheless we all feel
that the same underhand forces are fighting
against us, and estranging us from the supreme
power, by shaking its confidence in us. We
are hindered from striving to attain this union
with the Government, which, according to
the law of our new *régime*, ought to be the
essential condition of success and the pledge
of the peaceable development of our national
life. There it is that the greatest danger lies,
and it cannot disappear so long as the direction
of State affairs remains under the influence of
men who are *maréchaux de logis* and police
spies by their training and assassins by their
convictions. (*Prolonged applause from all
sides, and cries of 'Resignation.' From the
upper gallery a voice in ringing tones shouts,
'Assassins!'*) "

At the close of Prince Urussoff's speech
M. Vinaver mounted the platform and followed
to their logical conclusions the speeches of
the Minister and the previous orator. He

was dismayed by the apathy of the Government in face of a state of affairs in which the secret rule of the camarilla and Trepoff (the Star Chamber of Peterhof), so admirably described by Prince Urussoff, mocked at the fate of the country both before the face and behind the back of the Ministry. " Do you think it proper," asked M. Vinaver, addressing the Government, " to safeguard the life and security of our citizens by methods which smirch us with dishonour ?   As for me, I have for my task to watch over the lives of our citizens.   I am criminal even if I remain inactive and do not defend them, and you— you sacrifice their lives, and make of them a weapon of political propaganda."

M. Vinaver then drew a vivid picture of the policy of the "pogroms" for more than twenty years, which our readers already know.

"At that time," continued M. Vinaver, " M. Plehve was Director of the Department of Police, and when twenty years later the Ex-Director became Minister of the Interior and protested against the Kishineff 'pogrom,' a report was spread about a mysterious telegram sent from St Petersburg to the Governor of

the district.[1]   And the contagion, after the
Kishineff pogrom, spread itself over the whole
of Russia.   The Minister of the Interior con-
siders the fact that the officials of his
Department distribute broadcast proclamations calling for Jewish massacres, as is stated
in Boudogovsky's pamphlet, as only a simple
means of political propaganda.   When these
officials not only distribute the aforesaid
pamphlets, but in their reports inform their
superiors of their exploits, they are well
aware that it is an understood thing that
they will be favourably regarded.   They
constitute an absolutely unique institution,
and one which is outside all ordinary and
recognised governmental control.   It has a
secret existence, and possesses the right to
communicate with all subordinate officials,
from whom it receives direct reports, and is
able in consequence to direct all actions on
the spot by means of its secret machinery.
What does the Minister of the Interior do
when one of his officials circulates pamphlets
inflaming one section of the populace against
the other?   It has been stated here that
Boudogovsky had received a warning.   And

---

[1] Disclosed by the correspondent of the *Times,* and denied so
clumsily by Plehve and his assistant Lopukhine, that one can
readily believe that this sanguinary message urging the authorities
of Kishineff, as was afterwards done by Trepoff and Durnovo,
not to hinder the " patriotic demonstrations," was actually
sent.

Messrs Ratchkovsky and Timofeïeff, what did they receive? Were they arraigned in the Courts? Have they too been warned?

" Does the Minister know, and will he admit, that Ratchkovsky, on the occasion of his new appointment, received a donation of 75,000 roubles (£8,000)? (*Cries of ' Oh! Oh! Bravo! Bravo!' from the Labour Benches.*) Does the Minister of the Interior know that M. Timofeïeff, Chief of the Special Division of the Police Department, still holds office? The career of this man presents a certain interest, for he was legal adviser to the Prefect of Moscow, when the Prefect was General Trepoff; he was Director of the Special Division of the Police Department, when the Deputy Minister of the Interior was General Trepoff; he was Attaché (as he is still) to the Commandant of the Imperial Palace, when that Commandant is General Trepoff. (*General laughter.*) Ah well! Are Timofeïeff, Ratchkovsky, and the Minister of the Interior, Durnovo, who knew everything, of the opinion of the present Ministry, who hold and use their power to ensure the peace and welfare of the citizens? They know and they are silent, for they are the true authors of the 'pogroms.' Thanks to this silence and benevolent support, Boudogovsky is not the only Boudogovsky who has been produced. He shoots up in every corner of the country."

M. Vinaver, having told the story of Podgoritchani, the organiser of the last "pogrom" of Gomel, who was sent by Durnovo and Trepoff into another provincial town with the same powers, questioned the Minister as to the position of the Government after twenty years of such proceedings.

"This is not a governmental *régime*; this *régime* has but one name, anarchy. I think that the anarchy which ferments in the heads of young people, and is hidden away in out-of-the-way places, is a hundred times less dangerous than your undisguised fundamental anarchy. (*Loud applause.*)"

Need I also quote from the speech of M. Nabokoff, who gave the details of the "pogrom" of Vologda organised against the local workmen and the "intellectuals" by Captain Pychkine and the wife of the Zemsky Natchalnik (provincial magistrate), in spite of and against the Governor, the Prefect of Police and the Procureur. . . . The Governor Lodygensky has since resigned, being unable to assume the responsibilities created by Pychkine, who remains at his post, and is about to be rewarded.

Need I further quote the remarkable speech of the eminent *savant* Maxime Kovalevsky, stigmatising the secret mainsprings which are working in the neighbourhood of St Petersburg, independently and in defiance of the nominal Government; that of the generous Aladiyne, revealing the conspiracy of the murderers in high places against the movement towards freedom and against the Duma; that of Bondareff, a witness of the massacres of Volsk, of Balacheff and of Saratoff (at the time when the Minister M. Stolypin was governor), when, whilst the hooligans were plundering and pillaging the Jews, the Vice-Governor Knol was driving about in his carriage, acclaimed and saluted by the murderers with "Hurrahs!" which he acknowledged by a gracious smile, whilst continuing his drive?

It is unprofitable to go on with these quotations, since the speeches first cited state the case. The accusations made were recognised as accurate, the facts were established without any possible refutation, and the Duma drew their moral therefrom, by accepting the very moderate order of the day

presented in the name of the party of the
Freedom of the People by its Vice-President,
Professor Gredeskul.

The following was the resolution adopted :

"The Imperial Duma, after having heard the
explanations given by the Ministers of the
Interior and of Justice, and recognising in
the ' pogroms ' and in the wholesale massacres
of peaceable citizens which have taken place
and continue to take place in Russia, indubi-
table signs of a general organisation in which
officials, who remain unpunished, participated ;
considering that the explanations of the
Minister of the Interior evince the impotence
of the Ministry to check the afore-mentioned
occurrences, and show at the same time a
complete want of comprehension of the
conditions which render such occurrences
inevitable under the present *régime* ; recognising that only a ministry supported by
national representation can have enough
moral authority and power to control its
administrative subordinates and to remove
the irresponsible alien influences which lead
to the collapse of all authority and to anarchy
in the Government ; and concluding that so
long as there shall exist in Russia a ministry
which is not responsible to the national
representatives, the lives, honour, and liberty
of Russian citizens will not be safe from

violent and arbitrary treatment, and that the
immediate resignation of the present Ministry
and the transfer of power to a Cabinet enjoy-
ing the confidence of the Imperial Duma are
alone capable of saving the country from the
painful and rapidly increasing agitation, passes
to the order of the day."

CHAPTER XII

BEFORE dealing with the latest campaign of the " pogromists," I deem it necessary to add to the foregoing narrative and documents a few facts taken at random which illustrate and confirm them.

In the first place let us deal with the attempted pogrom at Sevastopol when Trepoff, Bogdanovitch and Co. endeavoured to reply by massacres to the Manifesto of the 30th of October, wrenched from the Government by the general strike.

" *A Demonstration financed by Trepoff*

" The Prefect of Sevastopol, Admiral Spitzky, received from St Petersburg on the 30th of October a telegram signed Trepoff, instructing him not to publish the Manifesto before having received the money for the purpose

of organising a patriotic demonstration. He
received the Manifesto, together with 60,000
roubles and a letter explaining to him that
the money was intended to provide for the
expenses occasioned by the organisation of
the patriotic demonstration, and recommending him to withdraw the police from all parts
of the town.

"Being much perplexed, and not knowing
which to obey, the Tsar's Manifesto or Trepoff's
orders, the naïve Admiral applied to the Mayor
of Sevastopol, M. Maximoff, for his advice.
They decided to publish the Manifesto, and
to keep the money in order to organise with
it a civil militia to protect the inhabitants.
The Manifesto provoked general joy, and the
workmen organised a pacific demonstration
accompanied by songs and the waving of
red flags. They went as far as the Totleben
Museum. There, from the top of the peri-
style, Dr B—— read the Manifesto, when
the Prefect of Police dashed up at full speed
with a party of Cossacks whom he ordered
to unsheath their swords.

" A bloody collision was about to take place,
when the commander of the district, Colonel
de Roberty, arrived shouting to the murderers
that to read the Imperial Manifesto was not
a crime, and ordered the Cossacks to quit
the town.

" Then the crowd, which included nearly the
whole of the population (about 30,000 people

Y

out of 36,000 to 38,000), went to the Boulevard
Maritime, where a monster meeting was held.
They elected 20 deputies to place before the
municipality the claims of the people, demand-
ing first of all the release of the political
prisoners. The Mayor, M. Maximoff, was at
first frightened, but he received the deputation after having removed his chain of office.
The deputies, however, asked him to put the
chain on again, inasmuch as they had to speak
to the official magistrate. In answer to his
evasive replies, a young girl deputy told him
peremptorily :

"'Mr Mayor, we have not come here to
lay a supplication before you : it is an order
the people are giving you, and they are
waiting.'

"M. Maximoff had to accede to the demand.
We know the rest—how the procession and
the meeting celebrated the Manifesto of the
30th of October, and how an abortive attempt
was made by the Governor of the prison to
frighten the people. A hitherto unpublished
detail is worth mentioning : the colonel of
the Bielostok regiment disowned the young
lieutenant who gave the order to fire from
the prison upon the crowd, and accompanied
to his grave the body of the mutinous sailor
treacherously killed before the prison when
the political prisoners were set free. It was
thanks only to the organised militia that the
hooligans were unable to perpetrate the

massacres which Trepoff's police had prepared.
Admiral Spitzky published an order of the
day thanking the militia, and acknowledging
that it was owing to their perfect organisation
that it was possible to avoid the massacres.
"Three days afterwards Admiral Tchukh-
nin returned from his cruise on the coast of
Asia Minor, disbanded the militia, and dismissed Spitzky."

The Popular Militia at Samara

The pogrom at Samara (city and province)
was prevented by the foresight of the inhabitants of the chief town of the province, which
borders on that of Saratoff. In the latter
province the "black hundreds," under the
benevolent eye of the Governor Stolypin,
and with the active assistance of the Cossacks,
had committed in the form of pillage, assault,
murder, and extermination of whole villages,
horrors exceeding those of the Kurds and
Bashi-Bazouks in Turkey. Having with the
authority of the Governor, M. Zasiadko,
organised a committee of public safety, the
population had thereby saved the town of
Samara from sharing the fate of Saratoff,

where the hooligans committed murders, and pillaged and burnt the stores, synagogues and houses of Jews, previously marked out for the purpose. The Committee organised public relief for the destitute, workless, etc., so as to prevent disorders. They persuaded the unions who wished to declare a strike to give up their idea in view of the alarming state prevailing everywhere. They did even more. We read, in fact, in the *Molva* of the 30th January 1906 as follows:

" During the first days of November (end of October, Old Style), when the ' black bands ' were still conducting ' pogroms ' in different parts of the country, the Committee heard that the Vice-Governor of Samara, M. Kondoidi, was causing a proclamation to be prepared in the printing works of the Government, appealing to the worst passions of the people.

" Having succeeded in obtaining a copy of this appeal, printed and distributed by the Vice - Governor, the Committee were able to satisfy themselves that the appeal was couched in the spirit of the ' black bands,' inasmuch as it contained an emphatic affirmation that the strikes and all popular movements in Russia proceeded exclusively from the Jews and the young students."

Considering the danger of such an official agitation emanating from the Vice-Governor, the Committee approached the Governor with a view to getting the Vice - Governor, Kondoidi, immediately dismissed from his office, and sent away from Samara. The Governor acceded to the request of the Committee, caused a proclamation to be posted up so as to neutralise that of the Vice-Governor, and the Vice-Governor "went away on leave," which fact the *Vedomosti* of Samara proclaimed so as to quiet the minds of the people.

Furthermore, the Committee through the medium of a delegation approached Count Witte to draw his attention to the unjustifiable action of the Vice-Governor, Kondoidi, supporting their statements by proofs and documents. M. Kondoidi was at once dismissed. But afterwards, when the Government thought themselves strong, the old order of things was reinstated, and it was the Governor, M. Kasiadko, who was relieved of his office on account of his kindness and liberal views. The 'black bands' fully appreciated the motives for the Governor's dismissal.

Amongst many other facts of the same description, I may mention the case of the Prefect of the Police of Kozloff, M. Lipko, who frustrated a "pogrom" prepared by the Vice-Governor of Tamboff, Bogdanovitch, the son of the principal author of the "pogroms," and also at Novozybkoff (see Appendix), and elsewhere. Bogdanovitch came to Kozloff to reply to the Manifesto (which he declined to read at the Town Hall), by massacring the Jews and the "intellectuals." Owing, however, to the resistance of the Prefect Lipko and the energy of the councillors and some courageous citizens, Bogdanovitch was obliged to read in full the Manifesto of the 30th of October. The "pogrom" was avoided, but M. Lipko was a marked man.

I must pass over the cases of Rostoff and Taganrog (where an exalted personage went himself to organise the massacres), and of the territory of the Terek in the Caucasus, where a military Governor was requested to organise a "pogrom" of Jews by a personage in such an exalted position that it was impossible for him to refuse. Nevertheless, this military Governor asked the said personage to have

him relieved of his office if he wished to insist
upon the organisation of a "pogrom." But
how rare have been those brave men who
were able to resist the requests, demands, and
even threats of Trepoff and Bogdanovitch,
and men like the Durnovos and their emissaries! And how numerous, alas, have been
the Neidhardts, the Kurloffs, the Kaulbars,
the Stolypins, the Chirinkines, the Chirinsky-
Chikhmatoffs, the Azantchevkys, the Slevtoffs,
the Stichinskys, and all the others trained
in the school of Plehve, Ignatieff and Co.!
Cities ruined and laid waste, their inhabitants
ruthlessly slaughtered, bear ample testimony.
to their number and their zeal.

These are the chief facts, but how many
more are there, of a less striking character,
which are of daily occurrence in Russian life,
and which render national existence a misery!
Let us quote at random from our daily papers.

We find in the *Hasman* the following
report:

"The advocate Chidlovsky, editor of the
Kharkovsky Journal, having been accused by
the Government of spreading false rumours,
made an application to the Court—

" 1. To call upon the Ministry of Foreign Affairs to produce before the Court the photograph of the circulars of the late V. K. Plehve addressed to the Governors of Kherson and Bessarabia, giving them instructions not to oppose the ' pogromists.' Copies of this historic circular are to be found at the offices of the *Times* in London.

" 2. To take legal note of the reports of Senators Turau and Kouzninsky containing authentic data showing the participation of the local administration in the ' pogroms ' of Kieff and Odessa.

" 3. To verify the telegrams sent by the Ministry of the Interior in the course of the month of October 1905, and especially a telegram sent by the Vice - Director of the Department of the Police, Ratchkovsky, ordering the administration not to meddle with the national conflicts which might arise amongst the inhabitants."

As an illustration of the probable action of the police in view of the forthcoming " pogroms," the *Retch* relates the following :

" The priest of the township of Salucce (in the district of Nejine, government of Tchernigoff), Father Veligodsky, was questioned by his parishioners as to whether there was any occasion to beat a certain Jew, who was the only one in the township, and very poor.

He made the following answer:—'We must not listen even if we are advised to do so, and even if the person who advises wears the police uniform. The Jew is useful to us. Furthermore, we must have pity upon him, and not strike him. He works for his family, and yet he remains very poor. He has not enough to eat.'

"The result of this speech was that the people took potatoes, bread, etc., to the Jew, whilst nobody in the town received either the policeman or the chief constable. Whilst looking out for lodgings, the latter came upon a peasant cleaning his yard. Exasperated by the insolence of the policeman, the peasant threw mud into his face. Then the policeman exclaimed: 'Ah, it is the priest who taught you that!' And he sent a complaint in due form alleging resistance to the authorities.

"A few days later the parishioners were surprised to hear that their priest had been imprisoned. Moved by the occurrence, they drew up a petition, and sent a telegram to Count Witte.

"Thirteen days afterwards Father Veligodsky was released, but by order of the Bishop Anthony was excommunicated and unfrocked. The clergy made an enquiry, and found nothing incriminating the priest, but the order remained in force, and at this very moment Father Veligodsky is in hospital, and his family and five children are without food or shelter."

Z

We read in the *Strana*, 6th (19th) June 1906:

" The compositor of the printing works of the *Journal of the Prefecture of St Petersburg*, Andreieff, has been imprisoned and sentenced to deportation by administrative means. The cause of the deportation is as follows:—On the 31st of April (13th of May last) proclamations of the ' black bands ' were brought to the printing office of the Prefect to be set in type. The compositors refused to set the same, giving as their reason for their refusal that they did not wish to take part in the distribution of proclamations sowing hatred amongst men. On the next day, that is to say, on the 1st (14th) of May, the compositors were dismissed from the printing works, and a few days afterwards Andreieff was arrested and sent to prison. After a fortnight's incarceration (without examination and without any definite accusation being formulated), he was informed that he would be deported for five years to one of the northern governments, by order of the Prefect of St Petersburg." [1]

The *Pout* of the 4th of May (21st of April) announced in a telegram received from Ekaterinoslav that the Bergman case was

[1] Launitz, an accomplice of Bogdanovitch, senior, and late superior officer of Bogdanovitch, junior.

fixed for the 10th of May. This Bergman, whilst in a crowd of Jewish workmen, threw some vitriol on the policeman Efimenko, which nearly caused a Jewish "pogrom." When arrested, Bergman said his name was Alexieff, and added that he was a member of the Public Safety Organisation, and an *agent provocateur*, and that in this capacity he had already repeatedly fired revolvers in order to provoke "pogroms." It was thus that at Minsk he fired (for fun) on the Prefect of Police, but "General Trepoff always interceded in his favour."

When we add these facts to all we know already of the history of the "pogroms," need we ask ourselves whether we require further documents and proofs to establish the guilt of the pogrom organisers ? [1]

[1] See Appendix.

CHAPTER XIII

THEY come to us, these bitter cries, from all parts of Russia, from Vologda, Murom, Tzarizyne, Wiazniki and Bielostok, where pogroms have recently taken place; and from Odessa, Kieff, Alexandrovsk, and Rostoff, in fact, wherever the "pogroms" were to take place, or the "black bands" were getting ready, assisted by Trepoff's agents, by the Generals on their rounds of inspection and by the police officials who are supplied with proclamations, with formulæ ready to be telegraphed to the Tsar, and with money—with French money.

Yes, at the present moment what we foretold, and what will be writ large in history, is being realised. The Government still maintains its army with French money, leading it against the whole nation, who have nothing but the moral and intellectual force of the Duma on its side.

The French money went straight to the murderers. The Caucasus, the Baltic Provinces, Siberia and the south, are invaded by reinforcements of punitive expeditions. Fresh and awful bloodshed is being prepared in the dens of Peterhof.

And in order to distract attention from all this bloodthirsty orgy, Trepoff and Co., still with French money, have flooded the provinces with their emissaries in order to organise, on the one hand, a so - called national petition against the Duma, and, on the other hand, "pogroms" against all Liberals and revolutionaries, and particularly against the Jews.

By their excess of cynicism and insolent audacity, the authors of this undertaking have themselves revealed it to the world. Having the nation against them, Trepoff and his black bands are reduced to the necessity of even drawing up the patriotic addresses at Peterhof, and sending them into the provinces, whence their agents send them back to Peterhof.

The official journal, the *Government Messenger*, which published nothing about the historical sittings of the Duma, fills its columns with so-called patriotic telegrams, little suspecting the effect which they produce upon the readers, considering that they are all worded in much the same terms. The following, according to the *Nasha Jizn*, which reproduces and collates them, is approximately the formula of these patriotic telegrams:

" If they (the members of the Duma) wish to work to help Thee and the people, let them work. But if they wish to play the part of leaders of our destiny, then remove them, and rest assured that the whole of the believing Russian people will support Thee. It is not a question of ruse or deceit, but merely of rising for Thy defence, to defend Thee who protectest Thy people, and herein lies our strength."

This is how the fate of the Duma is being prepared,[1] these addresses being further supplemented with requests—which are not only barbarous but anti-constitutional and disrespectful towards their Tsar — not to

---

[1] This was written before the dissolution of the Duma.

grant an amnesty and not to abolish capital punishment. If there is any hesitation, and if things are allowed to drag along in regard to the Duma, the more audacious and energetic becomes the preparation of fresh massacres. Alarming telegrams daily reach the members of the Duma, denouncing such preparations and imploring their intervention.

The passport offices are crowded with those who are able to go abroad — panic reigns everywhere. We receive letters from certain out-of-the-way provincial places, saying life is at a standstill; the black bands and the Cossacks alone are active.

Cries of alarm and cries of distress ring mournfully in our ears.

We bring them specially under the notice of Frenchmen who have given money to the murderers, and we submit to them the case of Bielostok, the first step in the new campaign which the assassins have prepared (see chapter xiv.).

Let us first of all deal with the origin of the patriotic telegrams and addresses.

The unbiassed newspapers give absolutely staggering details of the origin of these documents. Not to multiply examples, let us take a typical instance which we find in the correspondence addressed from the little town of Lipovetz to the *Retch* (see issue of 20th May (2nd June) 1906):

"The Justice of the Peace, M. Duchenke-vitch, notorious for his denunciations, in collaboration with other 'patriots,' such as Jdanovitch (Postmaster-General), Kvitnitzky (Assistant Inspector of Excise), and Chliahetko (Treasurer), laboured with all their might in the drawing up of the address of the 'Black Hundred.' All these chief officials incited the civic functionaries by every means in their power to sign the address by terrorising and threatening them. . . . In their search for 'faithful subjects' they had recourse to all kinds of pressure and intimidation which they especially brought to bear on depart-mental officials. . . . The President of the Court of Appeal, M. J. Tacievsky, the whole staff of the higher elementary school of the town, led by the head master, S. T. Guber-nartchuk, and even the marshal of the nobility of the district, P. M. Gudim-Levkovitch, refused to sign this telegram from 'faithful subjects,' *which, although drafted in the name of twelve thousand inhabitants, was only signed by fifty or sixty persons, of whom several were little boys!*"

In the same way the address of the government of Pensa was sent in by a police official against whom legal proceedings were actually pending for having tried to intoxicate the peasant delegates at the time of the elections to the Duma.

At Astrakhan, the patriotic address sent to St Petersburg in the name of a large section of the population was really forged by seventy local reactionaries. The local Press actually published protests against this address alleged to have been signed by thousands of citizens. One of these protests was signed by fourteen thousand peasants.

A truly characteristic occurrence took place at Pinsk in Volhynia. The chief of the district called together about a hundred peasants in a "tea-house," where he delivered in their presence a patriotic speech. The gist of the speech was as follows:—" The Government earnestly desire to give land to the peasants, but the Poles and the Jews in the Duma prevent it." Having made this speech, the chief of the district telegraphed a loyalist address to St Petersburg, which he said that he had been bidden to send by an assembly

2 A

of two thousand peasants. The same sort of thing has happened in other districts.

While this official agitation is proceeding against the Duma for the purpose of discrediting it in the eyes of the country and of foreign nations, a bold stroke is secretly being prepared against it. All the newspapers are full of revelations of the *military conspiracy* against the Duma, in which are mentioned all the officers of the Guard who particularly distinguished themselves by their cruelty at the time of the *repressive expeditions* to Moscow, and in the Baltic Provinces, etc. At the same time, and to put the matter in a nutshell, in the provinces the activity of "black bands," like the Union of True Russians and its "patriotic" branches, gains ground with a strength and audacity exceeding anything ever seen before. We already know the mental calibre of the "True Russians," but we will refer to it later in order to properly understand to whom the troops and police, acting under orders from *high quarters,* give their *active* support during the massacres of Jews and "intellectuals."

On   the   14th   of   November   last   the

Moskovskya Vedomosti published, on its front page, a bloodthirsty manifesto in the name of the Sacred Union of Popular Self-Defence, which opened in this wise:

" The Cross of Christ is the symbol of Love. The red flag is the symbol of blood. He who is for the Cross is with us ; he who is for the flag is against us. Let us unite in the name of Christ for the cause of Christ, for the Tsar, the Fatherland, the maintenance of order and a peaceful existence. He who raises the red flag raises the symbol of blood, but he who takes the sword shall perish by the sword. Behind us is the orthodox Russian nation, with us is the Christian army. For God, the Tsar, peace and the prosperity of Holy Russia."

Then followed a direct appeal for " pogrom " activity in the provinces, which could not but encourage the organisers and leaders of the "black hundreds" in their abominable work.

The following proclamation was published by the Patriotic Committee of Odessa:

" Brother Russians ! A sad fate has over-taken our Fatherland. This mighty Russia of ours is now racked with grief and anguish. Anarchy and despotism hold undisputed sway, and the name of the Tsar is dragged in the mire. Commerce is threatened, the price of provisions is rising, the people of Russia groan under their burden of misery.

" But the Jews, the people who are the cause of all this, are not affected by this wretchedness, because their richer brethren abroad send them sufficient help.

" Why did we suffer such defeat in the recent war ? Because we had two wars : a war without and a war within. And on whom devolves the chief responsibility for these troubles, if not on the Jews and the other alien races who scheme and who will profit by this general disorder to establish a Republic ? The other Powers surround us, like birds of prey, ready to swoop down upon us. Already they gloat over a Russia divided amongst them, under the pretext of defending their own countries. Brother Russians ! do not suffer your Fatherland to be engulfed ! Rouse yourselves and be men ! Defend with your last breath your Faith, your Tsar, and your country ! Russia for ever ! Down with the Jews ! "

At their official conference lately held in Russia, the " True Russians " adopted a resolution in which we find this clause :

" As for the Jews, they ought to be considered aliens in Russia. They should be debarred from holding any state or public offices. They should be deprived of all political rights, even of military service, which in their case ought to be replaced by a tax. All Government establishments should be closed against them. They ought to be hunted from all the organs of the Press, telegraph offices, and free universities; the right to buy or lease grounds outside the city should be taken from them! The Jewish Pale should be maintained. The discussion of the question of the equality of rights for Jews should be forbidden in the Duma."

A single aim, a single spirit directs all this anti - revolutionary agitation, although the outward signs appear to be different in different places. It is only by knowing a certain number of facts that it is possible to understand this unity and perceive that it had its origin in very high places. Besides, it is the only logical and plausible reason for the fact that after each "pogrom," and after each world-wide scandal that the "pogrom" provokes, the operations of which we speak continues as if nothing were wrong, as though Ministers had not promised to put a stop to the scandal, and had not sworn to conduct investigations, etc.

And so, while the late Ministry promised the Duma to see that the "pogrom" agitation was suppressed in the governments of Kieff, Podolia, etc., patriotic emissaries, saying that they were sent by the priests of Kieff, spread abroad the following proclamation (see the *Strana* of 27th June) surmounted by a black cross :

"Orthodox Russians! Many benefits have been promised you by the Imperial Duma, and you expect much — but do you know what it is preparing for you? The Duma promises you land, and to that end it will divide between you all the lands of the Treasury, the Tsar, the monasteries, churches, and individual landlords; and it has been calculated that if all these lands are taken from the actual owners and added to agricultural land and divided into equal shares among all the workmen, these would not be more than eight acres per head; consequently, if one of us possessed at this moment more than eight acres, the surplus would be taken from him and given to one who had less. Other members of the Duma have had a still better idea. According to their opinion all existing lands, including those of the peasantry, must be given up—and, still in the name of the Treasury, apportioned out

to the peasants, not in freehold lots, but on
lease. It is thus the Duma works in your
interests, but this is not all. The Duma
thought it would make you happy by granting you equal rights with other classes. That
means that you will no longer have your
mayors and your elected seniors, nor your
courts of justice nor your parish assemblies:
nothing of all which you have and which
other classes have not, but instead you will
be free citizens, and henceforth there will be
no nobles nor middle classes nor peasantry,
and all will be equal in the eyes of the Tsar
and the law as before God. All that would
be nothing, but the unfortunate part of it
is this: when amongst the Russian citizens
there are no more class distinctions, then the
Duma will decree that there must no longer
be national or religious distinctions either. It
will demand that the noble, the merchant, the
peasant, the Orthodox believer, the Catholic,
the Mohammedan and the Jew, shall all be
equal, that they shall all be Russian citizens
and enjoy the same rights. Then all the
miserable Jews who have no land (and there
are more than five millions of them in Russia)
will rise up and say, 'We have no longer any
moujik or gentleman, Russian or Jew. Now
there are only Russian citizens who are all
equal in the sight of the Tsar and the law;
consequently, when it is decided to divide the
land, give us poor Jews who have no land,

some as well, at the rate of eight acres each, and, since there are five millions of us, you must give us 40,000,000 acres.' This is the aim of our Duma and of its present members, whom the Jews or the traitors bought by them, the Russian democrats, have elected. Do not put faith in this Duma. It will do you no good. It is not difficult to rob the rich, but popular wisdom has always known 'that stolen goods bring no ease.' And it will be so. You may take land from the owners, but—you will make a mistake! It will fall into the hands of the Jews at the rate of eight acres for every infidel soul. There is your equality! There is the settlement of the agrarian question! Well, be on your guard, all you Orthodox believers, against the Jewish Duma. It makes you a soft bed, but you will find no comfort in it. It promises much, but it will not be you, Orthodox Christians, who will profit by it, but the Jewish ragamuffins, who will establish themselves on land wrested from the Treasury and the landowners. This will be the upshot of all the present troubles."

In this last proclamation, sown broadcast by the party of the Counter-Revolution, my readers, I think, will have the full measure of these dismal voices of the dying past, which in a last effort would drown the Revolution in blood, especially in Jewish blood.

I do not wish to linger over the other documents scattered throughout the country to which bloodthirsty newspapers such as the *Novoïe Vremya* of St Petersburg, the *Moskovskya Vedomosti* of Moscow, the *Russkaïa Retch* of Odessa give their support. We are already sufficiently edified and instructed. I will only quote one official document, the last and supreme proof that the Government, even after the terrible massacres of Bielostok, went hand in hand with the "Russian Patriots" who disseminated these pamphlets and organised the massacres.

This is the document, published by the *Retch* of 15th June (28th) 1906:

"*Circular*

"To all ispravniks, Heads of Districts, local administrations and committees and municipal offices.

Ministry of the Interior.
Governor of Minsk.
Government Office.
Section I., Bureau I.
June 6 (19) 1906, No. 3819.
Town of Minsk.

"In view of the report of the Minsk Branch of the Union of True Russians, dated 25th May (7th June) 1906, I order the ispravniks (chiefs of rural police), Heads of Districts, local administrations and committees and municipal

2 B

officers not to prevent members and presidents
of the Parish and rural sub-sections of the
Union from spreading amongst the people the
doctrines of this Union which are designed
to serve by legitimate means the Orthodox
Faith, the Tsar and the Russian Fatherland,
and which are set forth in the brochures and
leaflets published by the Central Council and
quoted by the patriotic papers.

F. J. Governor,
P. KURLOFF.
For the Vice-Governor,
JUZEFOVITCH,
Prime Minister.

" To the Editor of——"

Thus we find the Governor Kurloff, who
was arraigned before the Supreme Court of
the country for the massacres of October and
November at Minsk (after those of children at
Kursk), scandalously shielded by the Minister,
Durnovo, and as scandalously acquitted, continuing under another Minister, but under the
same Trepoff, a similar policy of " pogroms."

There seems to be nothing more to add to
this statement, unless it is to give a rapid
sketch of the tragedy of Bielostok, that last
drop in an already overflowing cup of blood
and crime.

CHAPTER XIV

BIELOSTOK

THE following letter from Bielostok, despatched on the evening which preceded the pogrom (31st May=13th June), appeared in the Vilna newspaper, *Der Weg*:

" The assassination of Derkatcheff, the Prefect of Police, made a profound impression on the local population.

" Sincere regret for such an excellent administrator is everywhere felt. The motive for the assassination remains a mystery. In the town it is thought to be the work of the hooligans, who have thus revenged themselves on the Prefect for refusing his permission to allow the pogrom to take place on the previous Sunday.

" The Jewish population in particular is greatly troubled and alarmed.

" The representatives of the Jewish community decided to offer a last tribute of respect to the deceased, and to lay a wreath upon his tomb. But the Assistant Chief of Police, Chérémetieff, declined to accept it at the hands of a Jewish delegation.

" ' We can accept,' said he, ' no wreath from blood-suckers and murderers. You imagine that your wreath will hide the blood that has been spilt. If you carry your wreath before the coffin, you will see what will happen in a few days.'

" These words have produced a terrible impression on the Jews. A deputation, composed of the banker Goldberg and of the doctors Reigorodsky and Iserson, started at once for Grodno, and returned to-day with the Governor's reply. The Governor assured them that Chérémetieff is a trustworthy official, who always says what he means. It is not his business as Governor to investigate the private sentiments of his subordinates, but he will take steps against the threatened pogrom.

" The whole population looks forward to tomorrow with anxiety, being the day fixed for the two processions, Orthodox and Catholic. Those who can are flying from the town, and those who remain are uncertain what will happen."

Here, too, is an extract from a letter despatched from Bielostok by a correspondent of the *Nasha Jizn* on the 6th (19th) June. :

" At the beginning of last week a report was

spread that some emissaries were inciting the peasants to enter the city on the following Thursday. Many of the soldiers sought out their Jewish friends and advised them to take refuge in flight. A soldier of the Kazanski regiment bade farewell to a Jewish friend, and besought him with tears not to remain in the city until Thursday, quoting a speech made by the Colonel of his regiment: ' It is you who defend the Tsar and the country, and the Jews seek your destruction. They have combined together to exterminate you, and I formally authorise you, in the name of the Government, to take your own measures between now and the 21st.' "

I know nothing about the Colonel in question, but this is what the *Retch* of the 1st July (18th June) tells us as to the moral character of Chérémetieff, the Chief of Police, and the principal hero of the " pogrom " of Bielostok. He received regularly every month a bribe of twenty-five roubles from the Jews of Bielostok, but when he demanded a loan of one thousand roubles, he was refused, thereupon he had recourse to threats. Formal complaint of his conduct was made to the Prefect of Police, who informed the Governor of the facts. An official enquiry was made, and the

offence was proved. For punishment Chérémetieff was transferred to Grodno, the chief
town of the district, *but he very shortly
returned to Bielostok.*

I will spare my readers the revolting
particulars of the massacres at Bielostok on
the 14th, 15th and 16th of last June, and
of the horrible cruelties perpetrated even by
officers upon the unfortunate Jews. At a
given signal a panic was created in the very
midst of the religious procession, and there
ensued a series of brutalities too inhuman to
be imagined. Skulls were fractured, bodies
mutilated, men and women burned alive,
children trampled to death—brutalities which
equalled the crimes of Kishineff and Odessa.
But it is idle to recriminate when a bogus
official telegram, which the local authorities
have themselves declared to be falsified,
described the concerted signal of the agitators
as an anarchist bomb.

I will now pursue the history of the
preparation of the "pogrom" as ascertained
by the official enquiry of the Duma and
by the private investigation of M. Klimkoff
of the *Retch* (27th June = 14th June).

The acting Prefect of Police, Radetzki, had observed a few days before the massacre that some of his commissaries and constables had misconstrued the orders he had given with regard to preventive measures against the expected "pogrom." He thereupon sought counsel and support from the military authorities, although at that time the state of siege had not been proclaimed. This appeal was received in such very bad part by one of the assistant chiefs of the garrison that on the day before the "pogrom" M. Radetzki, concluding that the *Governor was in complete unity with the military authorities, sent in his resignation on the plea of "ill-health."*

At an extraordinary meeting held on the day of the "pogrom," and attended by the Governor, the police and military authorities resolved to employ the same decisive measures as those which had proved so effective in the repressive expeditions to Moscow and the Baltic Provinces. The Governor then washed his hands of the whole affair, and took his departure abruptly for Grodno, while the obstructive Prefect of Police was succeeded by a trustworthy man named Matzevitch. It is a fact that the gendarmes who, whether disguised or not, certainly took part in the massacres, were superintended by a general of gendarmerie sent expressly for the purpose to Bielostok.

The Government had been informed of the existence of a very well-organised system of self-defence on the part of the Jews, and this necessarily influenced their plans. Moreover, there was no racial hatred between Jews and Christians (such as existed, for instance, at Kishineff, where nearly all the Moldavians, headed by their famous leader Kruchevan, himself a Moldavian, were anti-Semitic), so that, in the absence of reliable forces of hooligans, the Government was forced to call upon the regular troops. Thus Suraj-skaïa, Arguentina, and Pesskine, the quarters most densely populated by Jewish artisans, suffered but little from the " pogrom," because neither the hooligans nor the regular troops would venture into these quarters without a reinforcement of artillery, and this reinforcement fortunately did not arrive at Bielostok until the " pogrom " was at an end.

For this reason the outbreak at Bielostok is known as the military pogrom. Not only the police but the gendarmerie and the troops were engaged in it.

At a meeting of officers held towards the end of May, it was decided that at the first sign of disturbance among the "revolutionaries"—meaning the Jews — the most relentless measures would be employed. Through the agency of non-commissioned officers and adjutants, the soldiers were specially instructed as to dealing with disturbances. Their minds were inflamed against the Jews, who were accused amongst other things of having murdered a man of the Kazanski regiment, and of planning the death of all soldiers by poison or the knife. It was, however, specially through the medium of print that the propaganda was carried on. The Uglitski, Kazanski, and Vladimirski regiments were only permitted access to anti-Semitic newspapers such as the *Novoïe Vremya*, the *Znamea*, and the *Den*, but the authorities soon found that the appeals of the *Den*, owing to their exaggerated character, were losing their effect on the minds of

2 C

the soldiers as a body. Upon this they
published proclamations of an official character, and therefore all the more dangerous,
always bearing the words "authorised by the
Censor." Here is one, dated Odessa, 27th
January (14th January) 1906, bearing the
imprint, "Printing Office of the General
Staff of the Circonscription of Odessa."

"Have you any notion, my brothers, what
'Zionism' means? It is an ingenious in-
vention of the Jews, who once had their
own Zionist kingdom thus named after
Mount Zion. They lost it, and it is now a
Turkish territory. Ever since then they have
wandered over the face of the earth seeking
a foreign country which they might appropriate
and call it Zion. Hence the cry : 'Long
live Zionism!' Already they have hoisted
their standard here in Russia; it is a *red
standard*, and by fraud or bribes they have
collected round it a group of obscure persons
who are plotting to destroy our Batiuchka-
Tsar, and to set up a Jew or a Zionist in his
place. After that, my brothers, as surely as
they crucified the Christ, so surely will they
abolish the religion of Christ in Russia.
"My brothers, you will never deliver your
country into the hands of such a ferocious
enemy! Spurn his schemes of a Jewish

kingdom. When the devil offered all the kingdoms of the earth to the starving Christ in the desert, did not He reply: 'Get thee behind me, Satan!' My brothers, follow His example, and with one voice exclaim: 'Down with Zionism! Down with the red flag! Down with the red liberty of the Jews! Down with the liberty and fraternity of Jewish rebels!'

"Down with the new foes! Russian soldiers, Forward, forward to the attack!"

By such means was the train laid for the Bielostok massacres and for the atrocities perpetrated by the soldiers and gendarmes, while their commanders cheered them on with shouts and laughter. Then the Government sent to Bielostok for the purpose of making enquiries, one of the highest dignitaries of the Court, the Equerry, M. Frisch. But do you know what was M. Frisch's idea of conducting an enquiry? He passed over in silence the share which the troops took in the pogrom. Whenever this question was raised by an eye-witness, M. Frisch and his agents silenced him and corrected his statements, and from this man the Tsar learnt the "truth" of the massacres at Bielostok. He no doubt read also the *Novoïe Vremya*, which exults over the reprisals against the Jews, and the *Government Messenger*, which on 4th July published the following *communiqué officiel*. This, in spite of the cynical falsehoods it contains, reveals the counter-revolutionary object which the instigators of the massacre are aiming at in attempting to exterminate the whole Jewish community :

"Disturbances took place at Bielostok on 14th June, resulting in the death of 82 persons (7 Christians and 75 Jews) and the wounding of 78 (18 Christians and 60 Jews), and in the plundering of 169 Jewish dwellings and shops, representing a loss of about 200,000 roubles.

"In order to ascertain the exact cause of the disorders, the Minister of the Interior despatched M. Frisch, member of the Council of Ministers, to Bielostok. The report supplied by this official and other information received by the Government furnish the following details :

"'Bielostok, which possesses about 100,000 inhabitants, of whom 70 per cent. are Jews, has become of late years the chief centre of the revolutionary movement in the western provinces. The criminal activity in revolutionary circles there increased rapidly in 1905, and led to a series of murders and outrages perpetrated on the officials and the local police.

" 'A period of tranquillity succeeded the proclamation of martial law in September 1905, but immediately on its abrogation (1st March 1906) disturbances recommenced with renewed vigour.

" ' Between the 1st March and the 1st June, judicial enquiries were held with respect to 45 crimes committed by the terrorists against private individuals as well as against Government officials. The criminals could in very few cases be traced, no eye - witness being willing to come forward and risk the vengeance of the accused. A succession of such crimes threw Bielostok into a state of panic, and the murder of Derkatcheff,[1] who enjoyed the universal esteem of Jews and Christians, raised public exasperation against the disturbers of order to the highest pitch.

" ' The police were now quite demoralised. They had lost so many of their comrades by assassination, injury, or flight that it had been found necessary to enrol men without any special training.

" ' The excited state of the inhabitants and the disorganisation of the police created conditions in which serious disturbances could arise from the slightest cause. Thus on 14th June an audacious outrage led to an out-

[1] It is a fact that M. Derkatcheff was assassinated by an ex-police officer on account of his defence of the Jews.

burst of indignation on the part of the whole
Christian population.　During a procession on
that day explosives were thrown from two or
three places and revolvers fired, with the result
that the soldiers came upon the scene and fired
at the houses whence the shots proceeded.

"'Almost simultaneously a Jewish "pogrom"
broke out with extraordinary fury, no distinction being made between innocent and
guilty.

"'The course taken by the "pogrom" can
only be determined by the official enquiry,
which is being conducted with the utmost
expedition.

"' For the present it is only possible to
establish the fact that the "pogrom" was
mainly carried out by a small section of the
rural and urban population, and that in most
cases the pillage was arrested by the troops,
which were promptly summoned.

"' By seven in the evening Bielostok had
been freed from the plunderers, and patrols
were parading the streets.

"'On the following day the "pogrom" broke
out afresh.　At noon the revolutionary
organisations commenced a series of attacks
on the troops, which did not cease until the
night of the 17th.　(See Appendix.)

"' All facts so far ascertained by the enquiry
have formed the basis for measures taken in
order to re-establish a normal state of affairs.

"' With regard to persons implicated in the

"pogrom" and their accomplices and instigators, the Courts will use all the power with
which they are invested in order to effect the
arrest, trial, and punishment of such persons,
and the Government on its side will do everything in its power to inflict just punishment
on all private individuals who have had any
share in the horrors of Bielostok.

"'The Government repudiates with indignation the reports circulated to the effect that
the Bielostok pogrom took place with the
knowledge and connivance of the local
authorities or troops. The Government deem
it their duty to express their conviction that
the cause of the deplorable occurrence is
chiefly to be sought in the activity of the
local organisations.'"

The Government are, however, very much
mistaken if they suppose that the civilised
world will prefer to accept their version rather
than that given by the Duma Commis-
sion, which corroborates and amplifies the one
given by us. Moreover, the most influential
both of the English and French journals—
the *Times*, the *Matin*, and the *Temps*—
estimate this official statement at its true
worth.

The unfortunate victims themselves, though
still in terror of their lives, sent the follow-

ing telegram to the authorities, as a protest against the false report made by General Bader —one of the superior officers guilty of complicity in the massacres—who adopts in his report the version first given by the assassins (the anarchist bomb, etc.):

" We notice that in the report, sent by General Bader to the Minister of War on the 10th (23rd) June, on the pogrom and its causes, several of his statements are incorrect. This can be proved by consulting the official papers and by recalling the counter-statement made by the Governor of Grodno. Consequently we demand that a special sitting of the Duma should be called to consider the question and make out an accurate official report." (See Appendix.)

The sitting of the Duma on 4th July was accordingly occupied with the Bielostok incident. Before giving a short account of this memorable sitting, I will relate what passed at an interview granted by M. Chtchepkine —one of the deputies who served on the Commission of Enquiry sent by the Duma —to the St Petersburg correspondent of the *Temps*.

*" The Version of the Duma Commission
of Enquiry*

" One of our St Petersburg correspondents
has had the good fortune to obtain an interview with Professor Chtchepkine, Constitutional Democratic Member for Odessa, who,
with two of his colleagues, was sent to
Bielostok to enquire into the events of last
month. Our correspondent writes as follows :
" ' The member for Odessa began by describ-
ing the state of mind in Bielostok.
" ' Ever since last October a continuous
agitation has been kept up against the
Jewish population of the town. This has
been, no doubt, intended to counterbalance
the Socialist propaganda of the workmen's
organisations. Rumours were spread of the
atrocities supposed to have been committed
by the Jews, and open allusions were made
to the bombs which they were said to intend
using on the occasions of religious processions,
at Christmas or Easter. Had it not been
for the energetic resistance of M. Derkatcheff,
superintendent of the town police, who reduced his staff for the occasion, a " pogrom "
would certainly have taken place on Whit-
sunday, 3rd June (21st May). This resistance
just a week later cost him his life. His
assassination was immediately attributed to

2 D

the Jews, whose zealous supporter he had
always been. From that and other indica-
tions it was clear that a "pogrom" was
imminent.

"'The Governor of Grodno, when informed
of the situation, evaded responsibility.* He
declared that nothing could be done with
regard to the police officer Chérémetieff, who
was one of the instigators of the massacre,
and merely assured his interviewers that there
would be no pogroms on 14th June (1st
June). He said, however, that if a single
shot was fired the troops would use their
weapons. It is stated that this particular
Governor looked upon volleys as the only
effectual means of stemming a revolutionary
movement.

"'Turning to the description of what
occurred on the day of the massacre, the
Professor asks me to correct the word "bomb"
which appeared in the telegrams. There was
no bomb in the strict sense of the word, but
there was a contrivance filled with some sort
of explosive. The noise caused by the explosion was so inconsiderable that a great
part of the procession did not hear it. This
explains why those persons at the head of
the column did not stop, but were marching
on undisturbed, when the police interfered and
compelled them to halt.

"'I will not dwell on the terrible details which
my distinguished informant communicated to

me. They are only too well known. The unfortunate schoolmaster Aïnstein, slaughtered
with his wife and two elder children, and who
was found with enormous nails driven into
his skull, affords eloquent testimony of the
horrible and useless cruelty with which the
massacre was perpetrated.

" ' With regard to the part played by the
Army, we are bound to say that the soldiers
looked on unmoved whilst the slaughter
proceeded. If surprise was expressed at their
attitude, the officers explained, in the most
amiable manner, that the only duty of the
troops was to support the police, and that they
could only interfere on the formal request
of the civil authority. The latter, in the
persons of subordinate police officers, only
sought the aid of the military against the
unfortunate creatures who had the extraordinary audacity to defend themselves rather
than be butchered without a struggle.

" ' Finally, it would seem to be the case—
M. Chtchepkine looks upon the statement as
true, although in view of the enormities which
it relates it is to be most strictly reinvesti-
gated — that a general and a colonel, both
subordinates of the Governor, advised their
chief and the Commandant of the Police to
keep themselves out of sight and let things
take their course, with the result that the
head of a whole administrative district and
the Mayor of the city offered no opposition

to a military gang eager for violence, thirsting
for blood, in open revolt against the legal
authorities, to whom the sage advice was
given to sit still and mind their own business!
This surely constitutes the essence of Government anarchy.

" ' In conclusion, the Professor informs me
that the members of the Duma look upon
the massacres of the Jewish population by
the police and the troops as ordinary murders,
and that they are about to demand that a
large number of persons shall be brought
to trial in consequence.' "

We now come to the discussion in the
Duma which finally exposed the official mis-
statements.

The following account of the sitting is
taken from the telegrams published by the
London *Times*, the *Matin*, and the *Echo
de Paris* on the 6th and 7th July 1906:

" St Petersburg, 5th July.

" This afternoon's sitting was entirely taken
up by the Bielostok pogrom. M. Arakantzeff, reporter of the Investigating Committee,
spoke for nearly two hours. The galleries
were crowded to suffocation. M. Stolypin,
the solitary occupant of the Ministerial benches,
took copious notes. M. Arakantzeff's report

was delivered in quiet, sober language and in a low voice, which only heightened the thrilling horror of the narrative. 'They had,' he said, 'the names and addresses of all the witnesses upon whose evidence the report was based, but many of those names could not, for obvious reasons, be made public, at least not so long as the present administration remained at Bielostok and the city was under martial law, and until these conditions were changed, he contended it was quite impossible for the Government to ascertain the truth by an official enquiry.'

" M. Arakantzeff supplemented his report by reading a telegram from doctors at Bielostok certifying that a bullet had been extracted from a woman who was supposed to have been struck by a bomb. This finally disposed of the allegations in the official report that a bomb was thrown at a procession. The only bomb was thrown in Sourazhskaya Street by hooligans who tried to extend the pogrom. It hurt nobody. This street was notoriously a terrorist stronghold, yet neither soldiers nor police ventured thither. If reprisals are evoked by revolutionaries, how was it that Sourazhskaya Street was left alone, while other streets were pillaged and the inhabitants massacred? The official report says that the troops were constantly fired upon by Jews from windows. 'What,' he asked, 'were the losses among the troops? Three wounded!'

and he had the evidence of an officer that
these men were accidentally wounded by their
comrades.   The official reports say Jewish
revolutionaries bombarded the central Police
Station from a house which was burned, and
in which eight or nine revolutionaries were
found killed.   This house could be no other
than the house adjoining the sawmills.   It
was physically impossible to fire from there
at the police station.   He had shown in the
report the real circumstances of this un-
provoked butchery.

"'Why,' he asked, 'were the massacres not
stopped on the second day, when M. Stolypin
claimed to have sent orders to that effect?
The history of the Bielostok massacre was
only a counterpart of the whole infamous
policy of stirring up racial hatred, whereby
the old *régime* hoped to perpetuate its own
existence.   Finland. Poland, and the Caucasus
were other examples.   The authors thereof
had not scrupled to degrade the army to the
rank of butchers and to besmirch the revered
name of the Emperor.   Let the whole world
know that the pogroms were not the work
of the Russian nation, but of the so-called
Government of Russia.   It had deceived and
demoralised the Army and the Country, but
when the eyes of the Army were opened it
would see through the imposture, and then
woe betide the enemies of the Russian nation.
(Applause.)

" ' The inhabitants of Bielostok had anchored their hope of salvation and justice upon the Duma. He would ask the Duma to honour the memory of the victims by standing up.'

" The whole House then rose in solemn silence."

The following telegrams appeared in the *Echo de Paris*:

" We have published the official report of the Bielostok massacres. According to M. Frisch, who conducted the enquiry on behalf of the Government, a long and searching investigation is necessary in order to ascertain exactly what caused these sanguinary incidents, and who was responsible for them. At the same time, the Government repudiates indignantly the reports which have been circulated to the effect that the pogrom took place with the knowledge and connivance of the authorities and the troops, and it has announced that the origin of these deplorable events must be attributed to the action of certain local organisations.

" The Duma who, as we know, had sent to Bielostok certain deputies to investigate the facts, has in its turn published the report of its representatives. From this it is clear that in the opinion of the Duma, the police were responsible for the murders. The massacres were organised by a secret agency with or without the knowledge of the authorities."

The report of the Duma is as follows:

" The Report

"St Petersburg, *5th July.*

"For several days before the 14th June, a rumour was current at Bielostok that a pogrom was being planned.

"There seemed to be some connection between these rumours and the assassination of the Chief of Police, Derkatcheff, a crime still shrouded in mystery. Derkatcheff had been on bad terms with the inspector Chérémetieff, a man detested by the Jewish population on account of his violent methods, and whose removal Derkatcheff had tried to bring about.

"Previous assassinations of police officers had inflamed the police against the Jews, who were suspected of having had a share in them. On the other hand, the 'Union of True Russians' proclaimed on all sides that the Jews were the foes of the State, that they alone were responsible for its internal disorders, and that in consequence they must be attacked. The agents of the police were only too ready to echo threats and accusations.

"Shortly before the pogrom two camps

were formed.   On one side were the police
and the black bands; on the other were the
Jews, and all those who sympathised with the
Liberal movement and these were looked on
by the police as enemies of Russia.   The
existence of the Bund and of an anarchist
organisation are an open secret, and both
are imputed by the police to the Jews.

" The black bands took the necessary steps
to excite the soldiers.   On the 12th June
certain adjutants were ordered to announce
to the soldiers that Orthodox and Catholic
processions were arranged to take place on
the 14th, that the Jews would throw a bomb,
and that a pogrom would follow.   There
was not a single Jewish soldier among the
troops despatched to Bielostok, for care had
been taken to leave all men of that race
behind.   It is therefore abundantly clear that
the pogrom was no chance occurrence, but
that it had been arranged beforehand."

The report recalls the interview already
mentioned between the police inspector,
Chérémetieff, and the Jewish delegates who
wished to place a wreath on the coffin of
Derkatcheff, and continues as follows:

" Kister the Governor emphasised, for the
benefit of the Jewish deputation, the hatred
felt for them by the soldiers and the police.
He added that if during the funeral ceremony

2 E

a single shot was fired, he would without
hesitation give the order to fire upon the
town. He declared, however, that he would
hold himself responsible for what took place
on the 14th June, if not for subsequent
events. General Bader was equally convinced that it was the Jews who threw the
bomb.

"On the morning of the 14th June,
while the Orthodox procession was entering
Institute Street, some shots were fired from
a neighbouring house. A witness states
that whizzing was heard in the air, that
the sacred objects were thrown down in a
panic, and two persons were found to be
wounded.

"The soldiers appeared and opened fire
on the suspected house. They arrived so
promptly upon the scene that the crowd
had not time to disperse after the explosion.
A second bomb was thrown while the
procession was passing the bazaar.

"The bomb was apparently meant to drive
off the riff-raff, who were arriving in crowds,
and who did, in fact, disperse at the sound of
the explosion. The soldiers and police again
opened fire on the neighbouring houses, and
somewhat later the mob sacked a chemist's
shop; this was the beginning of the pogrom.
Police officers and loafers together broke open
and pillaged the shops, while the soldiers who
followed them swept the streets with their

fire in order to drive away the Jews. This firing on an invisible foe lasted from the Thursday till the Saturday. If a Christian passed in the street there was no firing, but if a Jew appeared he was received with a shower of bullets. On the Friday the police began to ransack the houses in their search for revolutionaries. Jews were pursued and murdered in the streets. Bodies of soldiers marched through the town, guided by police, who pointed out upon whom they were to fire.

" A ragamuffin had merely to shout ' Jew,' and the bullets whistled after the fugitives.

" The plundering and the rioting then slackened somewhat. The police and the troops were busy putting to death all whom they could find. To satisfy the army some pretext was necessary, and one was quickly found. A report was spread with amazing promptitude that an Orthodox priest had been murdered, that the same thing had happened to a Catholic *curé*, that the Jews had fired upon the holy images, and that a woman had been put to death. A journalist, too, was found, a petty official from Grodno, by name Stukalitch, who telegraphed officially that the Jews were committing atrocities. Many officers, believing these stories, vowed vengeance on the Jews. Two officers meeting a band of loafers in Bazar Street, concerted plans with them, and pointed out the street where they could begin operations. A company of soldiers followed and prevented any one from entering the street or interfering with the work of the mob.

" Hardly had the massacre begun at Bielostok when a mob assembled at the railway station and laid violent hands upon all Jews who were going or arriving by train.

" On the 14th June, the Governor of Grodno came to Bielostok, and after remaining a short time in the town, and somewhat longer at the railway station, returned to Grodno by special train. His presence at the railway station in no way checked either the soldiers, the police, or the roughs. The latter saw, on the contrary, that their conduct was approved, and continued their assaults under the eyes of commandant, officers, gendarmes, and soldiers, who looked on unmoved and encouraged the mob. It was a most brutal man-hunt. On the Thursday an officer of gendarmes told a crowd of hooligans that it was useless merely to murder a few wretched Jews at the railway station, and that they had much better go into the town and pillage the shops and attack the Jews.

" A major, who happened to be there, declared that the Jews must be put to death, and on the 15th June the number of murders was greatly increased."

The report goes on to specify the large

number of instances in which Jews were cruelly ill-treated, and even killed. It asserts that when these horrible details were brought to the notice of the Governor, that high official merely replied that the fault lay with the Jews who had fired shots and thrown bombs. The report then emphasises the premeditated nature of the massacres, which partook of the nature of a punitive expedition similar to those which have taken place in the Baltic Provinces and Siberia. With respect to the conduct of the Governor, it is proved that that official knew beforehand that the massacres were being planned, and that he took no steps to prevent them.

" When the members of the Duma, Yakubson and Scheftel, on the 15th June implored the Minister of the Interior to put a stop to the massacres at Bielostok, the Minister replied that he was on the point of telegraphing the necessary orders, but in spite of this a great number of Jews were murdered between the afternoon of the 15th and the morning of the 16th June.

" These facts show that the massacres were organised by a secret agency with or without the knowledge of the authorities. Further, the military authorities had handed over the town to the police and the troops. But who, on the 14th and 15th June, had transferred the powers of the Governor to the military authorities? This is a question which must be explained by the War Office."

Annexed to the report are a number of documents containing the detailed evidence of the charges which it makes.

The correspondent of the *Echo de Paris* further writes :

"The report was read in the Duma by M. Arakanteff. He declared finally that the Government was guilty, and that, for his part, he had no confidence in the result of the judicial enquiry. The Russian nation had never approved of the pogroms. The Government had already corrupted the army, which was what the Russians held most dear. But the eyes of the army were being opened. When it realised the horrors it had been forced to commit, woe to those who had corrupted it, and turned it into a wild beast. The speaker asked the deputies to stand up, in honour of the memory of the victims of Bielostok.

"The whole Duma rose." (See Appendix.)

The Government could have got out of

the Bielostok affair with more or less dignity,
if they had confessed the truth and thrown
the responsibility on the local authorities, or
on the "occult power." Instead of doing so
they joined hands with the assassins, and with
the "occult power." They are, therefore,
utterly dishonoured and disqualified in the
eyes of the whole civilised world. The Duma
did not fail to point out the dishonour, for
the Commission decided to put a question
to the Ministry, as the following telegram
shows :

"St Petersburg, 5th July.

"At the afternoon sitting, when the report
on the massacres of Bielostok had been read, the
Committee requested the Duma to endorse
an interpellation to the Minister of the Interior
asking whether legal proceedings will be taken
against the Governor of Grodno and the
Bielostok police for inactivity or approval and
participation in the *pogrom*, and to ask the
Minister of War whether he is acquainted
with the fact that the local military authorities
at Bielostok arbitrarily usurped the functions
of the Governor and police master and assumed
their duties, also whether he is aware that the
troops at Bielostok were from the 14th to the

16th June placed under the orders of inferior police officers, and, acting under their instructions and under the instructions of private persons, shot down peaceful inhabitants, and whether the guilty are to be prosecuted."
— *Times.*

Meanwhile the Government gave the final proof of its culpability and dishonour in the following telegram:

" ST PETERSBURG, *5th July.*

" According to a telegram from Bielostok (dated yesterday), the Mayor, M. Malinovsky, has been relieved of his functions by the Governor-General, because he intended to call a special meeting of the municipal Duma to deny the statements contained in General Bader's report on the massacres of 14th June."
—*Matin.*

CHAPTER XV

CONCLUSION

"Solitudinem faciunt: pacem appellant."-—Tacitus.

THE documents we have cited, especially the proclamations and official reports (see chapters ix. and x.), and the facts quoted to corroborate them, must lead every just and lucid mind to the following conclusion.

There is a power in Russia, working in the Tsar's name, and holding in its hand the army, the police, the secret police, the gendarmerie, and the administration. It employs these forces for what it calls *the pacification of the country, and for committing every kind of outrage upon peaceable citizens, especially on the Jews and on the intelligent element in Russia*—upon the majority of the nation that is, for of this the Duma is a living and absolute proof.

General Trepoff formed the nucleus of this power; a sinister figure, who has been connected with every outrage against the Jews, from the famous Moscow expulsions to the massacres of to - day. With Trepoff, and over him, we find General Bogdanovitch, the friend of Nicholas II. (see chapter vi.), Count Ignatieff, inventor of the "pogroms," the always maleficent Pobedonostseff, and *who else*? The question is obvious, for every one understands that Trepoff and Co., in the face of universal hatred, in the face of public opinion throughout Russia and the civilised world, could never retain the authority surrendered to them by the Tsar, unless some mysterious powers, in the immediate imperial circle, protected and upheld the bandits. What are these powers?

This book rests strictly on documents, and I would bring no accusation that I cannot support with irrefutable proofs. But, as a conscientious historian, I must chronicle the echoes of common rumour, which, as our work has proved in many a place, are so often the forerunners of documentary proof, the revelation of facts, and the exposure of the truth. What are these mysterious forces? Is it the terror of the self-interested, who see nothing in this tragedy of a nation but a question for the police; who have handed over the destiny of a great country to the men Prince Urussoff has stigmatised as "spies by training, and assassins by conviction?" Was Trepoff supported by a feminine influence? I would not stoop to the gossip of the Court whispered in society, but this is no question of a back-stairs intrigue; I ask it because it concerns the lives of millions of human beings.

Is it a certain Grand Duke, very closely related to Nicholas II., and now a member of his immediate family; the famous over-thrower of Witte in his struggle with Plehve? He is indicated in the letters of two correspondents, both well-known and distinguished writers, S. Persky, in the *Aurore*, and Sergueievsky, in the *Humanité*. In the latter, on 29th June, we read, amongst other things, the following:

"I have still to mention a very serious matter. M. Urussoff, an old member of the Witte - Durnovo cabinet, whose speech last Friday, on the regular organisation of massacres by the Government, produced so great a sensation in the civilised world—M. Urussoff, I say, forgot, or was afraid to inform the Duma of the atrocious fact that one of the anti-Semitic proclamations, published by the secret printing office of the Department of Police, bore these words: 'Passed for printing. F. Trepoff.' So it is the powerful favourite of the Court, influential alike with men and women—who has sent forth, coldly and knowingly, this most characteristic appeal to assassination. *It will be useless for the camerilla to deny the fact*: there are persons who ask nothing better than to be summoned before the court, that they may fling this accusation in the face of the gallant Trepoff. And the cause of the attack of asthma that struck down M. de Witte so suddenly—that very diplomatic attack of asthma mentioned by M. Urussoff in his speech — must be sought for *in the background and in high places.* They are somewhat similar to the reasons which caused the Earl of Portsmouth's resignation. But I will speak of this another time; those who are interested in it will lose nothing by waiting. . . . "

Is it the Grand Duke whose name is openly uttered in the lobbies of the Duma?

I ask these questions, and am certain that before long they will receive clear and distinct answers.

In the meantime, thanks to this protection, Trepoff [1] and his band have quite an army of irresponsible officials under their orders— Durnovo, Timoféïeff, Ratchkovsky, Kurloff, etc.—who, in this twentieth century, in face of a civilised world, organise and carry out with impunity concerted massacres "such as history never before recorded in the annals of any people," as the noble Mirbeau says, in a letter that I shall presently quote.

Yes, they are powerful, these murderers, owing to the support of the throne, or of its advisers—the same thing—but above all, they derive strength from the attitude of the powers that are called civilised. Such an attitude deserves to be scourged, and the historian will not fail to do it from a double point of view—from that of morality, and from that of humanity. This can be said best in the words of a great French writer, who, when I asked him to speak at a meeting, organised to protest against the

[1] See Appendix.

massacres, honoured me with the following
reply :

" MY DEAR FRIEND, — You must excuse
me from being with you this evening, for
my health is still indifferent; you know
I shall be there in spirit and thought, that
my soul is full of mourning, and overflowing with anger—powerless, alas !—for these
last crimes, these last atrocities of expiring
Tsarism.

" I wish to ask a question on a subject
which greatly troubles me.   When a horrible
murderer kills his wife and his mother, and
butchers his children in his own home, do
the neighbours stand on ceremony about
entering the house, breaking in the door,
and rushing on the murderer, on the pretext
that the place belongs to him, and that he
is acting within his inviolable rights as a
proprietor ?   I think not.

" Ought Europe, then, and the world, to
continue looking on impassively at the terrible
crimes committed every day in Russia ; crimes
such as history never before recorded in the
annals of any people ?

" Is it permissible—I do not understand
diplomacy, but I know what humanity is—
is it permissible for Europe and the world,
under pretext that Russia belongs to the
Tsar and his band of cut-throats, and on
account of I do not know what inter-imperial

and inter-royal conventions, to leave this unhappy people without help in the hands of this bloodthirsty homicidal maniac, possessed with the fury of massacre and destruction, and drunk with fear and blood?

" Are loathing, anger, and justice extinct?

" Has humanity ceased to exist? Is everything at an end, and have we nothing left to chronicle but the bankruptcy of civilisation?

" I know it is impossible now to stop the liberating march of the Revolution; that it is conquering towns, villages, the lonely huts, the land, and the people. . . . But until the day — now near, I hope — when it will be completely victorious, how many more crimes and heart-rending ruins, how much more bloodshed!

" And all this for a man, for a murderer who cannot resign himself to give up wallowing in the blood of his people, and fastening his teeth in their flesh!

"OCTAVE MIRBEAU."

This indignant cry of a noble heart does honour to the nation to which it belongs. Anatole France and the *Friends of Russian Freedom* unite with it in bearing witness for a France whose official representatives have maintained a lamentable attitude during the blood-stained crisis of Russia.

The practical side remains to be considered ; the side of those interests of civilisation that are common to all European States, the entirely material interests. I said, at the beginning of this book, that the scandalous position of a civilised Europe supporting with money, not the people struggling for liberty and justice, but the brutal power of the murderers, was based on a mistaken calculation. The question is, Will civilised nations much longer suffer the centre of massacre and abominable crime called Tsardom, to continue a work of destruction that, in the end, will poison the air of Europe, and make it reek with blood ; that will corrupt the new morality of humanity, freed with so much labour from the barbarity and the darkness of the Middle Ages ? The question is, Will Europe allow a return to the Middle Ages— the paradise dreamt of by Russian Tsardom— will she renounce legality in her politics, the modern methods of discussion and conflict, inaugurated by a triumphant capitalism and a rising socialism ; and, instead, hand over the West to fire and sword ? For the West will succumb to the contagion, if the violence and murder of the last two years are not put an end to in Russia.

But I will press the question still further home. Leaving on one side all the considerations that just touch, but do not really affect, the subscribers to the new Russian loans, I ask them, are they really so sure of the solvency of a Russian Government of which Trepoff was the chief support? I submit to them the striking words of Anatole France. I cannot better conclude this historical essay of a great contemporary drama, than by quoting the following extract from a speech made by that great thinker, at a meeting organised by the *Société des Amis du Peuple Russe*, on 30th June:

"One day or another the Government of the Tsar will make a fresh appeal to us for funds. It will borrow, under some ingenious and roundabout form (for it is fertile in resources for obtaining money), and probably it will not even wait for the complete payment of the last loan. Patriot financiers will not be wanting among us, who will respond to the appeal for the sake of the alliance, and in consideration of large commissions. Will the Government of the Republic authorise

2 G

this loan, when the preceding one has been
so badly taken up, that a third, perhaps half,
is still in the hands of speculators, who, owing
to the fall caused by the news from St Petersburg, are able, at every liquidation, to crush
the market with the weight of their depreciated
shares? We know very well under what compulsion the present Ministry consented to the
disastrous transaction of 1906. They did it
of necessity. They were forced into it by a
long succession of errors and mistakes, for
which they were not responsible. They signed,
under pressure, and with regret. This we can
affirm. If they denied it, we would affirm
it again. We would tell them: We do not
believe you, for you are honourable men.
But how long will they continue yielding to
the demands of a debtor who is more exacting
than any creditor, and who threatens to fail
as soon as any appearance is shown of ceasing
to support his debt? An alarming menace
this, it must be admitted—a truly sinister
menace when one remembers that in the
Russian budget the loan is the largest and
safest of the ordinary receipts; and that, should
this receipt be wanting, bankruptcy would be
inevitable. At the present moment the
situation is critical. Will our great financiers
and our rulers dare to increase the danger,
in order to turn it aside? Citizens, it is not
a question of knowing if Russia is solvent.
Hidden and in raw material, she possesses

one-sixth of the riches of the world. That is
more than enough to serve as a guarantee
for fourteen milliards; fourteen quite happy,
well-fed milliards, which can both hope and
wait. The question is, will her present government remain solvent? Many say it will.
Many believe it will. A still greater number
hope it may. A few say it will not, and
they are of those who do not make mistakes,
because they do not allow themselves to be
corrupted. The Government of the Tsar has
failed in authority, honour, reason, and
humanity. After all these bankruptcies,
financial bankruptcy is near and certain. For
the future the owners of Russian stock should
only count on the government that will
liquidate the huge bankruptcy of Tsardom
and bureaucracy. If we cannot say what
this government will be, we can at least
discern beforehand a few of the elements of
which it will be composed. We already
know the political groups, the social parties,
which, raised up by the Revolution, will be
called to the august and heavy task of repara-
tion. Now all these parties, as at present
organised, all these groups, from the most
violent to the most moderate, workmen,
peasants, *bourgeois*, intellectuals, are unanimous in declaring that the new Government
will accept all loans contracted before 1906,
and will pay the interest in full; but they
will not accept loans contracted since the

hour when Tsardom entered into conflict with the Russian people; loans raised by the Autocracy to use against the nation. The *Retch* newspaper, liberal organ of the majority in the Duma, wrote in similar terms on 10th (23rd) June. It said : 'The Government has thrown this new burden of a loan upon the shoulders of the people, in order to procure arms against that same people against the public will. As long as the present Government remains in power, as long as the Duma has not supreme control over the finances, that assembly will repudiate any new loan.' That is what is published by the official organ of the Duma. Let our fellow-citizens at last have ears to hear. They are warned : a very evil day may come for them, if they lend money again to the Russian Government, in order that it may shoot, hang, massacre, pillage at will, and kill all liberty and civilisation throughout the length of its immense unhappy empire. Citizens of France, give no more money for new cruelties and follies; give no more milliards for the martyrdom of countless people. By refusing to do so, you prove yourselves the friends of Russia. Russia has never, I know, been so dear to all that is best in the French nation as now, when she suffers, fights, and dies for her liberty. At this tragic hour, on the eve of one of the greatest revolutions of the world, let her receive homage from the sons of the men of '89 and the year II. And while we wait for our Republican Parliament to send a brotherly salutation to the Taurida Palace, we, simple citizens, united by a common sentiment of universal brotherhood, offer our homage and good wishes to the victims of Autocracy."

These words may be addressed to every European, to the whole of civilisation. Reflect upon them. I can add nothing to the authority of their speaker. But as a trustworthy and accurate historian, I ought to say that *I know* that Anatole France before uttering them had sought information from the great financial authorities of Paris; that when he speaks of the *compulsion* under which the present French Ministry acted, he speaks with full knowledge of his subject, and I ought to add that his final allusion to the *silence* of the French Parliament is only an echo of the sadness that wrings the best hearts in France when they think of that silence of their deputies, so strangely at variance with the humane utterances of the Parliaments of America, Great Britain, Austria, Italy, and Australia. . . .

Yes, on the day when Europe and America raise their voices against Tsardom and draw tight their purse - strings, the massacres in Russia will cease, even before the inevitable triumph of the Revolution.

APPENDIX

Vide PAGE 11

THE thesis of M. Allemand, entitled "Les
Souffrances des Juifs en Russie et le Devoir
des Etats civilisés" ("The sufferings of the
Jews in Russia and the duty of civilised
States"), after its refusal by the Faculty of
Law in Paris, was only accepted by a special
commission, assembled at the Ministry of
Public Instruction, under the Presidency of
the head of the Law Faculty at Lyons.

I have to thank M. Allemand for his
courtesy in putting at my disposal his book,
which, I repeat, is quite a remarkable judicial
work. It is above all interesting with regard
to the question of interfering in the affairs
of another country, a question which is
agitating all parliamentary centres of civilised
countries, especially since the massacres of
Bielostok.

It was, in fact, only after the Kishineff
massacres in 1903 that the Government of
the United States raised its voice, and it

was only after the scandalous official proclamations and the massacres of Bielostok that governments and parliaments were moved, with the exception of France (officially, be it said) and Germany.

The Government of the United States took the most courageous attitude; and the English also distinguished themselves in this respect. Sir E. Grey in particular exercised an historic influence, and his name will live in Russia for the speeches he made in recognition of the Duma as one of the official authorities of Russia.

It is interesting to consult the books of V. Bérard: " Le Tsarisme et l'Empire russe"; G. Bourdon: "La Russie libre"; G. Verdène: " Ceux qu'on méprise"; "La Revue" of M. Finot, who has published some remarkable studies on Franco-Russian finances (1905-6), "Le Memorial diplo-matique," "Les Cahiers de la Quinzaine" (December 1904), "Les Pages libres" (*passim*); and above all, the book by M. Léo Errera: "Les Juifs russes," containing the remarkable preface by Mommsen upon the "resuscitated Torquemada."

Vide PAGE 32

Count Ignatieff's Policy

Count Ignatieff endeavoured to turn the revolutionary movement upon and against the Jews. To justify his action, the famous Chief of Police Sudeïkine, with the traitor Degaïeff, published in the supplement of No. 1 of the *Narodnaïa Volia*[1] (St Petersburg, 20th July 1883) a perfidious article entitled "à propos des Troubles antijuifs" (reproduced in the *Bibliothèque historique russe*, vol. vi., on "La Littérature de la Volonté du peuple," by B. Basilevsky). They relate in this article the gruesome details of the anti-Jewish troubles at Ekaterinoslav in the month of July 1883, and distinguish the Jews from the Israelites, whilst at the same time, to cause confusion, Marx is quoted as saying that the Jews, having suffered unhappiness and persecution for so long, concentrate in themselves, and reflect all the vices of the times ; and Taine is quoted as saying that "the French Revolution was inaugurated with massacres of the Jews." I do not know which of the police agents was the author

[1] See the details of the treachery and intrigue of the police spies Sundeïkine and Degaïeff in M. E. Petet's account of "A Russian Bastille" in the *Humanité* of 2nd and 3rd July 1906.

2 H

of this article, which was intended to justify Ignatieff. But I do know that when Chebaline, a real Revolutionist, the manager of the secret printing press, received this article from the hands of Degaïeff, to be set in type, he protested against it. However, Degaïeff quieted him by saying that it was "the Executive Committee which had decided to publish the article." Needless to say that it was Degaïeff who, in this matter, represented the police and Ignatieff, and it was Chebaline who protested in the name of the true Revolutionists of the period.

Vide PAGE 76

The Last Massacres of Kishineff

The *Novosti*, a Liberal paper, publishes the following description of these events:

"A great misfortune has again fallen upon us. Our town has once more become a prey to the invasion of hooligans and Bashibazouks, who formed a plan of destroying our city by fire and sword.

"As was the case all over our immense Russia, the general strikes found an echo with us, and from the 16th (29th) of October all the artisans, workmen, and Jews went on strike. The strike remained peaceful on the 16th to the 18th October, and order was not disturbed by the strikers. Then bands of hooligans began interfering with passers-by, and molesting them. Matters were in this state until the 18th (31st) of October.

"On the morning of that day, the news of the Manifesto granting a Constitution to the people spread through the town. An enormous crowd immediately invaded the editorial offices of the local papers, waiting for telegrams relating to the Manifesto. Towards nine o'clock in the morning, M. L. Vihuroff, the chief editor of the paper, *The Life of Bessarabia*, appeared at the window of the office where his journal is published, and read aloud the Imperial Manifesto. The enthusiasm of the crowds baffles description. Thundering hurrahs filled the air, and the multitude crossed Puchkine Street towards the Alexandrovsk quarter.

" It was there that the first systematic extermination of the demonstrators by the police and the troops began, with the result that a number of Jews were wounded, some seriously and others slightly, and these were sent to the Jewish hospital.

"Nevertheless, the 18th of October was comparatively calm, and ended with numerous meetings ' in the cause of Liberty.'

" On the morning of the 19th October (1st November) rumours of bloodshed were rife. The writer of these lines was told that ever since the morning thousands of hooligans, with a band of anti-Semites at their head, assembled at the Oschoufflinskaia Square for the purpose of organising a meeting against the Jews, the ringleaders calling upon the crowd to rise against the Jews. An officer of the local police named Vassilieff spoke in the same strain, with the result that by ten o'clock in the morning a crowd composed of a thousand people, headed by the anti-Semites and the officer Vassilieff, rushed towards the Alexandrovsk quarter in the direction of the cathedral with the savage cry: ' Let us do for Witte ! '

" Arrived at the Mikhailovskaïa Street, the crowd

of patriots fell upon a party of Jews. Clamorous shouts resounded: 'Down with the Jews!' At the same moment provocative shots were heard, no one knew whence, and they served as a signal for the attack on the unfortunate Jews. The cries of the Jews who were struck and wounded filled the air, and the injured were carried off by tens to the Jewish hospital.

" Eye-witnesses of this bloody attack on the Jews by the savage, brutal crowd, declare that they recognised commissaries and agents of police in disguise, striking the Jews with their swords.

" Blood flowed down the streets all the day of the 19th. The Jewish hospital was already crowded with killed and wounded Jews, and it was in vain that the heads of our Jewish community called at the house of the Governor Kharusine, begging him to interfere.

" The Governor was deaf to the appeals of the Jews, declaring that the Jews alone were responsible for what had happened to them.

" During the day the Governor, the Vice-Governor, Count Tatichtcheff, the Procurator of the Court, the Prefect of Police, and Vassilieff, the officer of the Police, condescended to visit the Jewish hospital with the seeming intent of learning the number of killed and wounded. But as some of the wounded received these gentlemen with vehement and well-merited reproaches for the bloody attack under the very eyes of the police and the troops, the Governor and his suite hastened to depart, and after that none of the authorities visited the hospital. After the departure of the Governor some shots were fired at the hospital, and caused a terrible panic among the sick and wounded.

" It was only with great difficulty that the hospital doctors got the prefectoral administration to have the Jewish hospital guarded by the soldiers so as to prevent a further attack.

"In the meanwhile the horde of hooligans continued with mad fury their brutal exploits of pillaging and demolishing in every street the apartments and shops of the Jews.

"It was thus that Schach's very ancient bookseller's shop was pillaged and burnt down, as well as Krassilstchik's jewellery shop and many others.

"On the following morning, the 20th October, there was placarded everywhere an announcement from the Governor Kharusine in which, among other things, he warned the population of Kishineff that any house from which a gun-shot proceeded was to be immediately bombarded by cannon. This was simply an appeal to the instigators to provoke revolver shots from the houses of the best-known Jewish notabilities, so as to compass the complete destruction of their dwellings by bombardment. And indeed, towards midday fatal gun-shots suddenly rang out from the richest Jewish houses in the Alexandrovskaïa Street, and at about two o'clock the bombardment of the houses belonging to E. Galperine, Elie Braunstein, and Z. Spivak commenced. Moreover, the soldiers fired upon the branch office of the Industrial Bank of Southern Russia, as well as on a great number of private houses, killing or grievously wounding the unfortunate inhabitants. The number of Jews killed (men, women, and children) during the two days, from the 19th to the 20th October, was twenty-nine, and as for the wounded they were reckoned by hundreds. It is noteworthy that the hooligans did not operate in the lower part of the town, because the moment the hooligans appeared the 'samoborona' (self - defence) parties resisted them in a way which brought them to their senses without being opposed by the troops. In the upper part of the town, on the contrary, the troops supported the hooligans, letting them pillage and assassinate the Jews as they pleased. On the morning of the 21st October an order was posted up from our Archbishop Vladimir exhorting the pillagers to stop their sanguinary exploits. And as if by magic all was quiet immediately. The hooligans disappeared, and we were only left with tens of thousands of desolate Jews."

This description is interesting as coming from the scenes of the massacres. The facts are correct — the details and the figures can always be verified.

Vide CHAPTER XII

A party of barristers of St Petersburg and Moscow organised a Committee of Enquiry into the pogroms of October and November last. The results of this enquiry bear overwhelming proofs against the Government. This evidence, carefully verified and subjected to all kinds of tests, proves once more that it is the Government in the person of its direct agents that organised the massacres. We will only quote a few of the plainest and most simple testimonies from all these documents[1] which form a total of several large volumes of authentic documents.

The Pogrom of Novozybkof.—The Governor

---

[1] We have, moreover, in our possession documentary evidence from Rostoff, Odessa, Kieff, etc.

Khvostof was wounded recently at Tchernigoff.
He was the cause of one of the most terrible
pogroms in the town of Novozybkof in the
government of Tchernigoff. Among other documents we have the statements of Jews and Christians who were
witnesses and victims of the pogrom, and it
appears that the ispravnik of Novozybkof
organised the pogrom after a telegram from
the Governor of Tchernigoff. We give two
statements on the matter.

" *Statement of M. A. J., a merchant.*—On the 18th
(31st) of October the ispravnik Lobko-Lobanovsk
arrived very excited at the club one evening, and drawing from his pocket a telegram, which he folded in half
to prevent our seeing the first part, he declared that
he had telegraphed to the Governor at two o'clock that
afternoon about the demonstrations at Novozybkof (in
honour of the Constitution), and he had received a
reply from the Governor telling him that no Constitution had been granted, but that only the rights of the
Duma had been extended, and he added with much
agitation : 'I have a family, and I shall perhaps lose
my appointment, it is possible, but you will see to-morrow what massacres we shall have.'

" *Statement of a witness, M. J. P., a merchant.*
— On the 18th (31st) of October, at about eleven
o'clock in the evening, the ispravnik Lobko-Lobanovsk
arrived at the club looking worried, and said to
the members : 'Whoever imagined this Constitution?
There is no Constitution, no right has been granted,'
and he showed a telegram which he had received from
the Governor. In the first part of the telegram the
Governor blamed Lobko-Lobanovsk for the demonstra-

tion which he had permitted, and in the second part
he said that the rights of the Duma were only extended,
and it was Count Witte's mission to unify the Ministry.
'God is my witness,' declared the ispravnik, 'that it
is not my fault. I have little children : I may be
deprived of my appointment, but you will see what
will happen to-morrow. There will be massacres.'

"Considering that Lobko-Lobanofsk declared that
he had to announce to the people on the morrow that
there was no Constitution, that no rights had been
granted, and that he had to read the Governor's
telegram, I tried to calm him and beg him not to
announce anything to the people, and not to read the
Governor's telegram, assuring him that all would calm
down and nothing would happen. But he decided
otherwise.

" On the following day, 19th October (1st November),
at about eight o'clock in the morning, Lobko-Lobanovsk
collected together a crowd of roughs near the stone
shelves in the market-place, and when I went to my
horse, which happened to be there, I found him hoisted
up on a cab, from whence he had just read the
Governor's telegram, and was then saying : 'Gentlemen,
there is no Constitution, there are no rights. What
was said yesterday was invented by our enemies the
Jews, Doctor Ivanoff, and Bagoliuboff. Now you can
do what you like with them, you are given the right.'

"The crowd replied with loud hurrahs, and at once
began to strike the Jews who were present. I hastened
my departure and reached my house by side streets.
We learnt afterwards that the crowd then took to
sacking the shops, and striking and killing all the Jews
they met, and this with the aid of the ispravnik."

Vide CHAPTER VI

The *Mysl* publishes, and the *Nasha Jizn* (No. 479) reproduces, the following circular letter signed by Alexis Maximovitch Lavroff, Councillor of State and member of the Ministry of the Interior at the time of the publication of the said circular, dated 12th (25th) October 1905 :

"Our country is in danger; the press is in the criminal hands of the Jews, who lead the intellectual classes to unbelief, which weighs like a heavy nightmare on the people. Everybody is engrossed with his own personal interests, and has turned away from the common mother — Russia. The Jews take possession of all the forces of our political life. Gold, the earthly god of the blood-suckers, the promised Messiah, becomes omnipotent in their hands.

" Many Russian people, forgetting that in the days of misfortune Russia's strength was in autocracy, are now renouncing it. Where is the salvation of Russia? Where but in the union of men of duty and honour, who will lead the people against this enemy which oppresses Russia, as did Minine and Pojarsky when they roused it to the defence of their country.

" The aim of this circular is to wake the people to this idea. Come, therefore (and here was inserted in ink the name of the person to whom the circular was addressed), come and help forward the patriotic work of spreading this appeal. Help the people of Russia to become clear-sighted, and to free themselves from the yoke of the Jews, and a future that is worse even

2 I

than the present. If every man who loves his country,
every priest, every community responds to this appeal
to struggle against Jewry, then, like the drops which
wear away a stone, the good words will awaken the
people of Russia, and unite them in the struggle against
the common invincible enemy.—Yours, etc.,

(Signed)   A. LAVROFF."

Vide CHAPTER XIV

When writing the above chapter, I had not
seen the Russian text of the report of the
Parliamentary Commission sent to Bielostok.
Having since examined it, I find further con-
firmation of what I said about the massacres
of Bielostok. The preparations for the pogrom,
including the *mise en scène* of the provocation
in the midst of a religious procession, are all
clearly proved, as well as the culpability of
the superior authorities, both civil and military,
during the actual massacres.

There was pillage, devastation, a raid upon
the Jews who were killed in the streets, in
the houses, in the trains and at the railway
station, even in the restaurant, before the
eyes and with the approval of the officers
and officials. There was a systematic fusillade
surpassing even those of October in Odessa
and elsewhere.

Now follow the conclusions arrived at by
the Commission :

1. There was no race hatred, either religious or economic, between the Christian and Jewish populations of the town of Bielostok.

2. Undisguised hatred of the Jews existed only amongst the police, who imparted it to the troops, on the ground that the Jews were participators in the Liberal movement.

3. The pogrom was prepared beforehand, and this was known for some time by the administration as well as by the population.

4. The immediate pretext of the pogrom was also premeditated and prepared by the authorities, and it cannot therefore be considered as an outbreak of national and religious fanaticism.

5. The action of the army and the civil authorities during the pogrom was an open violation of the existing laws as well as of the regulations of 7th (20th) February 1906.

There was a systematic fusillade of the peaceable Jewish population, including women and children, under pretext of stamping out the Revolution. However, no revolutionary act—either on the part of the crowd or on the part of individuals — which could have given rise to such repressive measures, was proved to have taken place.

6. The civil and military authorities not only remained inactive before the pogrom, but in many cases, in the persons of their agents, they themselves were guilty of murder, mutilation, and pillage.

7. The official reports on the reasons, the pretexts, and the course of events (shots fired against the troops and against the Christian population, attacks by revolutionists, etc.) are contrary to the truth.

The Commission, therefore, is of opinion that the Duma should be asked to call upon:

(1) The Minister of the Interior, in order to ascertain if the Governor of Grodno and the officials and the police agents of the town of Bielostok have been called to account, some for their inaction during the pogrom at Bielostok, the 1st to 3rd (14th to 16th) of June 1906, and the others for having favoured the pogrom and taken an active and direct part in it.

(2) The Minister of War, to ask him if he knew (a) that even before the state of siege was declared in the town of Bielostok, the local military authorities removed the Governor of Grodno and the Prefect of Police from the exercise of their duties, which they took upon themselves in opposition to the existing laws; (b) that during the pogrom at Bielostok on the 14th to the 16th June 1906 the troops called to the town were put at the disposal of subordinate police agents. On their orders, and on those of private people, they fusilladed the peaceful inhabitants; and (c) have these delinquents been called to account?

The Commission must, moreover, add that the local population, already sufficiently

frightened, was completely terrorised by the
state of siege; and a regular enquiry into
all that has happened at Bielostok is only
possible on two indispensable conditions: (1)
the dismissal or removal of the local authorities
(civil as well as military), and (2) raising the
state of siege.

The reply of the Government to this
demand of the Commission of the Duma
was cruel, as is amply shown by the following two telegrams, published by the French
and English papers on the 10th of July:

" St Petersburg, 9th July.

"The papers announce that the commandant at
Bielostok has published an order thanking the troops
for their abnegation and devotion during the recent
revolts."

" St Petersburg, 9th July.

"The army organ publishes the Imperial thanks
to the troops for their 'splendid service, and their
glorious, self-sacrificing, untiring, just, and honest
devotion to duty during the Bialystok *pogrom.*'"—
Times.

And whilst people heard of these extraordinary "thanks," which would be astonish-
ing, were they not entirely in keeping with
what we have shown to have been the *rôle* of the
Government during the pogroms and after the
recall, by the Governor-General Bogaievsky,

of M. Malinovsky, the Mayor of Bielostok, merely for having convened a meeting of the Municipal Council in order to protest against the lies of the official reports on the pogrom, the debates of the Duma were continued.

The Roman Catholic Bishop, Baron Ropp, Deputy for Vilna, related many striking facts. One general, for instance, told him that the soldiers never fired on the Christians, but only on the Israelites.

The speaker expressed his conviction that the superior administrative authorities are always able to stop a pogrom if they choose to do so. On one occasion the Governor-General sent for the anti-Semitic agitators, and requested them not to prepare a pogrom. Their reply was: "You do not wish us to do it? Very good, we will do nothing."

The speaker further stated that a certain amount of ill-feeling against the Jews existed amongst the soldiers and the police. The cause of such ill-feeling was the excellent organisation of the Jewish community, which raises the envy of the Christians.

In conclusion, the speaker said that autonomy should be given to the western provinces, for, if not, riots were inevitable. The Central Government has always given a great deal of attention to the russification of the western provinces. It has even prohibited the formation of a moderate constitutional party in Vilna, under the leadership of the

Bishop, which party was hostile to anarchy.
The Government was, in that case, acting in
concert with the extreme revolutionaries.

Deputy Vinaver, in a long speech, quoted
facts based on documentary evidence, proving
the participation of the Central Government
in the massacres of the Jews.

M. Vinaver asserted that the massacres were
deliberately provoked by the representatives
of the bureaucracy. "M. Stolypin," he said,
"admitted before the Duma that several
thousands of proclamations were printed at
the Ministry of the Interior, 'in order to
stimulate the patriotism of the troops.'
Hundreds of thousands of such proclamations were issued from Komissaroff's printing
press."

The speaker then read several extracts from
such proclamations, inciting to the massacre
of the Jews, and "of all enemies of the
State."

"The aim of the Government is to compel
the Jews to betray and to deliver up the
revolutionaries amongst them ; but those
revolutionaries are more dangerous to the
moderate Jews than to the Government.
The Jewish nation is not very numerous, but
their strength lies chiefly in their despair.
Their ally is the whole Russian nation,
indignant at the acts of cruelty and barbarity
which have been perpetrated." (*Applause
from the left centre.*)

Deputy Roditcheff, in an impassioned speech which met with applause from all sides, described the policy of the Government—a policy full of lies which would lead the country into unheard-of dangers. The speaker concluded by saying : — " We have appealed to the Ministers, we have begged them to resign, but they are deaf; they will not listen to reason, they do not hear the rumblings of the storm which is drawing near. There are already many distant rumblings, which will unite in a terrible thunderclap, which will devastate the land, and when the Government, in its terror of such a catastrophe, thinks of resigning, it will be too late."

Vide PAGE 229

Habeum confidentum reum

Then Trepoff himself spoke. The interview given by Trepoff to a representative of " Reuter's Agency," and published by the latter in all the newspapers on the 9th of July 1906, should be carefully studied.

His hatred of the movement towards freedom, and more especially his hatred of the Jew, whom he would show to Europe in the same light in which he has shown him to the black bands, is obvious in every word.

The following extract is the most striking proof of this:

"I am of opinion that everything in reason should be done, so as to restore order and to maintain it by peaceful means. If such means are insufficient, then we must have recourse to other measures. The great strength of the revolutionaries lies in the fact that they control the press. I will not deny the fact that the revolutionaries have won over nearly all our men of talent, and even if moderate newspapers were started, the editors would find no contributors.

"Moreover, you know that a certain number of Petersburg papers are in the hands of Jews, most of their editors are Jews, and the reporters are usually revolutionary agitators. You will see from this in what proportion the Jews [1] are represented in the Duma. Whatever you may say, the present revolutionary movement is in the main the work of Jews. The agitation against the Christians which they carry on is planned with wonderful cleverness, and they are past masters in the art of posing as the innocent victims of bloodthirsty tyranny.

"I confirm all that has been said in the Official Report [2] relating to the massacre of Bielostok. When Prince Urussoff spoke the other day in the Duma on the

---

[1] The number of the Jewish representatives in the Duma should be twenty, but it is only twelve, including converts, and most of them have not been elected on account of their being Jews.

[2] How can he confirm it? In what capacity? As an enquirer, or as the person who ordered it? What a cynical and imprudent confession!

2 K

question of the encouragement given by the Government to the massacres, he simply lied. His calumnies are the outcome of thwarted ambition, and when he was forced to make definite accusations he could only cite two cases of officials betraying the confidence which the Government had placed in them.[1]

"It must not be forgotten that the provincial officials are very often in a state of exasperation on account of the murders and other crimes, the instigators of which are known to them. One blames them, but how can one be surprised if there are sometimes reprisals ? "

The Ignatieffs, Plehves, Trepoffs and their friends believed, and still believe, that they can distort the truth with impunity.

But they are blind and ignorant.

In the meantime a second secret printing press has been discovered in the Police Department (*Vide* the *Petite Republique* of the 10th July), which prints anti-Semitic manifestoes. Panic reigns in all the communities within the Pale.

The following is a telegram from Odessa,

[1] Here is Prince Urussoff's reply which was published in the papers :

"St Petersburg, *9th July.*

"Prince Urussoff, interviewed on the subject of General Trepoff's statements, replied to his interlocutor :

"'General Trepoff has not spoken the truth. He would not have spoken as he did if he had known that Witte had an enquiry made in January last which led to the drawing up of a report which will be published in eight or ten days, and of which the revelations will constitute a Russian Dreyfus affaire.'—*Echo de Paris,* 10*th July.*"

published by the newspapers of St Petersburg on 1st July (18th June):

"ODESSA, 17th June.

"A person named Kahoff has been arrested to-day, who was distributing proclamations inciting to massacres of the Jews and intellectuals in Préobrajenskaïa Street. Half an hour after his arrest Kahoff's brother (Secretary of the Russian Union) dashed into the police station, threatened the head official with his recall, and openly upbraided the police for resisting the *service of True Russians*. He telephoned to the office of the Governor-General, to whom he complained of the conduct of the police. After that he was immediately received by General Karangosoff, and his brother was forthwith set at liberty!"

The Jewish population is terror-stricken, the more so as the report is spread that an attempt has been made on the life of Grigorieff, the Gradonatchalnik (Prefect of the town), and that the author of the attempt was an agent of the police in disguise, just as at Bielostok when Derkatcheff was killed. General Grigorieff was against pogroms, whilst General Karangosoff, the Governor-General and the notorious General Kaulbars, Commander-in-Chief of the Military District of Odessa, are, like Trepoff, in favour of a bloody attack on the Jews and revolutionists.

And, as a final denial to the allegations of Trepoff and Co., let us give this paragraph from the *Correspondance Russe*:

" A Declaration of the Revolutionists and Anarchists

" ST PETERSBURG, *5th July.*

" The correspondent of the socialistic and revolutionary paper *Golos* (The Voice) writes from Bielostok:—

" ' In the course of an interview which I have recently had with several representatives of the socialist-revolutionaries and of the two anarchist organisations " The Black Flag " and " Bread and Liberty," the following declaration was made to me :

" ' " We, Socialists and Anarchists, the representatives of the only organisations which carry on the Terrorist struggle, we declare that deeming our method of fighting to be indispensable under the present *régime,* and deeming the murder of oppressors to be a just punishment for their crimes, we have never dissimulated our acts, and we have never concealed ourselves behind the backs of others. We have met the enemy face to face without paling before their vengeance, and our enemies themselves ought to give us credit for this. We declare in the face of the whole world that no member of our group nor any single Socialist nor Anarchist has ever thrown a bomb at an Orthodox procession or ever fired a shot before the commencement of the pogrom. The very fact that we are Revolutionists would have prevented us from throwing a bomb or firing upon a peaceable crowd ; and we would not have done it in this case for the still stronger reason that we knew such a deed would provoke the pogrom wished for by the police.

" ' " We affirm, moreover, that we have never been the first to fire a shot during Thursday and Friday when the town had to submit to the firing of the soldiers under the pretext that the Anarchists were shooting at the public buildings. We only fired on the soldiers and hooligans when they attacked us." ' "

INDEX

261